OMG! You Met on the Internet?

OMG! You Met on the Internet?

How an online romance conquered
grief and depression while
restoring faith in a higher power

Donna Marie and John Peterson

Cascade Press

OMG! You Met on the Internet?
How an online romance conquered grief and depression while
restoring faith in a higher power
Copyright © 2017 by Donna Marie and John Peterson

ISBN: 978-0-692-83243-1

FIRST EDITION

Cover deisgn by Nick Zelinger.

Book design by Sue Balcer.

To lovers and seekers of all ages who want to meet that special person who offers intimacy, commitment and fun. It happened to us, it will happen to you. Don't give up.

Note to readers

"Don't give up."

Sounds trite, right? You've heard it so many times. Well-intended advice, in most cases. Maybe a little too casual, or glib, in other instances. But *advice*, nonetheless. Common words pouring out of the mouths of so-called experts: friends, family members, a lover.

Yet we were both on the verge of giving up on life when we met online. Those three little words, simple as they are, initially were solace for the losses we'd both experienced. Later, those same words became a balm, a soothing reminder that miracles happen.

OMG! You Met on the Internet? is our story of overcoming grief and despair in our Golden Years. As you'll soon discover, it is an improbable love story that to this day delights and confounds us. How did it happen? How could we be so lucky? Thank God it *did* happen!

In the early chapters we share texts from our online chats that were made possible through an experimental relationship-based website. We saved our chats and have not changed them much for this book. Instead, we preferred to keep the misspellings and, in some cases, grammatically incorrect phrasing and run-on sentences so that you might marvel at how keen, clumsy, and to be sure, desperate we were to communicate.

Despite our admittedly basic understanding of technology, as our romance blossomed we learned more and improved our skills. We remain active online and eternally grateful that the Internet and the advent of smart phones, with so many handy apps and functions, have given us so much. Innovative technologies assisted two complete strangers, who lived on opposite ends of America, to find each other and fall in love.

We want the same for anyone who is alone and doubtful. Don't give up. Believe. All is not lost. If it can happen to us, it can happen to anyone else who is ready and willing to engage with this amazing world in which we live.

Blessings,

John and Donna Marie Peterson

PROLOGUE

Saying "I love you" in Sin City

In the baggage claim area of the airport, a tall man in denim pants and a blue shirt walks past a vending machine that sells flowers. A moment later he back-tracks and stares at the florist's display, unsure, undecided.

Finally, he pulls out his credit card, thinking, *Why not?*

Then his phone rings. It's me.

Even before getting on the plane heading to Las Vegas, I was on cloud nine. In fact, I'd been high since my first conversation months before with my new seventy-two-year-old boyfriend. I couldn't wait to meet him in the flesh.

But while talking with my daughter Bonnie, who was my travel escort, I began to wonder. How was JP going to feel when he saw me in person for the first time, a sixty-seven-year-old woman being pushed toward him in a wheelchair? The passenger assistance was necessary because I weighed nearly three hundred pounds. My other less obvious flaw was that I had only one breast. Could I blame the man if he was disappointed?

Not that I hadn't been frank about my various problems as we got to know each other online. Once, I began a conversation by saying, "I need to tell you something."

"OK."

"I want to be *naughty.*"

"Fine with me."

"And I wear Depends."

I was also concerned about my reaction to him. What if he said something that irked me, or I didn't like his scent? And would I feel comfortable when we held hands and shared our first kiss?

Unfortunately, there was too much time to worry. Bonnie and I were supposed to land in Las Vegas at about 2 p.m. But our flight out of Rochester, New York had been delayed several hours because Air Force One had entered the air space, and all planes would be grounded until the President of the United States passed through.

Then our connecting flight out of Chicago was also delayed. That meant we would not arrive until about 9 p.m.

These annoyances only encouraged my natural tendency to doubt. If something was too good to be true, my mind would often whisper, "This is not going to happen, honey."

Yet each time I called JP on the smart phone he'd purchased for me he sounded patient.

"I'm not going anywhere, honey. I'll be waiting. Enjoy your flight."

He was always so calm, and such a gentleman, that I couldn't help but adjust my thoughts and accentuate the positive. Memo to Donna: There is no end to this story, only a beginning.

Every time his phone rings the man in blue stares at the display, smiling when he sees my name. He hopes this call will bring good news. *Not.*

Later, he'll tell me that every delay only made him more

nervous, worried, and excited. We had talked so much by phone he thought that he knew me well; we were comfortable together, even when discussing intimacy.

Yet secretly he feared that he might not be able to perform in bed. He had not been active sexually for several years and his doctor would not allow him to use Viagra due to other health concerns.

With time on his hands, he heads to the rental desk, retrieves our car and then drives to the hotel where he has reserved two rooms. He checks in.

After landing I considered getting out of my wheelchair and walking to meet JP. But that would have meant trekking from one end of the airport to the other. No way. I was exhausted from the delays and stopovers, and I couldn't wait to see my man for the first time.

Instead, a skycap pushed me toward the baggage area where we were all supposed to meet. I was wearing a big floppy hat like the one Julia Roberts had worn in the movie *Pretty Woman*-- a hat JP had bought for me. And I was on the phone with him as we tried to locate each other in the crowded terminal.

"Where are you?" he said.

"Right here."

Closer, closer. Our moment was near.

"I can't see you."

But I could see him. He stood about five feet away, so handsome, holding a single rose. Tears blinded me as the wheelchair rolled to within inches of him.

"I'm right here," I said.

He turned as I reached my arms up and around his neck and pulled him to me. Our first kiss was the sweetest and strongest I had ever tasted. We hugged; I didn't want to let go. After months of waiting we could finally inhale one another.

But one more moment was needed to consummate our relationship. We'd held off, deferred gratification, only singing it to each other on the phone with favorite songs, promising that the spoken word would be more meaningful when we could actually touch and look into each other's eyes.

"I love you, honey."

"I love you too."

1

JP

Lonely farmer: I recently lost my wife of 52 years and feel lost.
I am 72 years old and just need someone to write to thanks for answering

DL Saucy: what's your name I am donna

Lonely farmer: hi Donna my name is John

A week before meeting Donna online, I was having a lot of trouble sleeping. I would lay awake wondering about   the future. At my age, why go on?

Nothing in life prepared you for the experience of losing a spouse. The grief was unbelievable. I read somewhere that grief was the price we pay for loving. They got that right. I'd loved and then lost Shirley--my wife, partner, and best friend. We had shared everything together. She had worked by my side for more than forty years as we developed a small farm in the state of Washington and then sold it to buy a larger spread. Both farms had been successful and provided for our family's every need.

But since her death I had no idea what lay in store for me. My life seemed directionless, and I had nothing to occupy my time. My farm went on without my involvement, because I'd retired years before and now leased the land to a local farmer. I still had some yard work to do, and I had to maintain the grass runway for my airplane, but so what? I did those tasks with a heavy heart, just going through the motions of life without really living.

Maybe I should sell everything and move closer to the city. It was on my mind, because I was so isolated, surrounded by my fertile but silent acreage. I couldn't talk to the trees, or sing with the birds and the bees. It was odd not having anyone to play cards with or watch TV. The little things that are so fulfilling when you share them with someone you love.

And I cried a lot. Sometimes I'd walk through the house in a daze recalling everything Shirley had done to make us a beautiful home, and I couldn't believe that she was gone. It didn't seem real. Even when I tried to work on her last will and testament and other legal matters my mind couldn't focus and function. So, at great expense, I turned most of it over to my lawyer. *Here, you deal with it.*

One thing I did accomplish was to take our wedding rings to a jeweler and have them hooked together. Everlasting love.

My grief was also affecting my health. I'd lost weight because I didn't have an appetite since Shirley passed, and my blood pressure decreased, which allowed me to stop taking most of my high-blood pressure meds.

"I think it's all the result of my depression," I'd told my doctor after sharing my complaints. He suggested a prescription drug to lift my spirits, but I declined because if it were reported to the Federal Aviation Administration they would not renew my pilot's license at my next physical examination. Flying was my last refuge. I couldn't give that up.

Two weeks after Shirley's funeral, I was playing with my cell phone, trying to keep my mind off things, when I stumbled on a membership website that helped complete strangers meet and used an online chat tool to type real-time conversations. Despite the fact that my sweet granddaughter had agreed to stay with me when my adult children understandably had to get back to their own lives, I was lonely. So I signed up, chose *Lonely farmer* as my handle, and began to explore a whole new world.

Looking back, I'm confident that something spiritual was guiding me. It was an intervention. I have no other explanation for how and why my life could change so swiftly and throw me onto a see-saw of utter joy and wrenching guilt.

While scrolling through the site, I found a sixty-seven-year-old woman who tagged herself *DL Saucy*. The name certainly grabbed my attention, and the profile was interesting so I decided to contact her. I had no idea what to expect. I just felt like I needed to talk to someone.

> DL Saucy: John is a very popular name where you from
>
> Lonely farmer: Washington state and you
>
> DL Saucy: New York it's very warm here now
>
> Lonely farmer: Here too
>
> DL Saucy: Do you have air-conditioning I'm so sorry for your loss John did you love her a lot do you mind talking about it or if you do just tell me
>
> Lonely farmer: I did love her a lot and I don't mind talking about her and I do have air-conditioning

Each time we signed on we shared more and more personal details.

> Lonely farmer: Donna do you have any kids if yes what are their ages.
>
> DL Saucy: two daughters 45 and 42. Five grandchildren two great-grandchildren.

Lonely farmer: that's great are you close to them? You won't believe this but I have seven kids six were my wife's together we have 17 grandchildren and 13 great-grandchildren.

DL Saucy: oh I believe it and that's awesome and yes I'm very close to my whole family.

Lonely farmer: that's good because family is so important.

She was so easy to talk to, and I enjoyed her sense of humor. Like when she asked if I socialized much or had hobbies.

Lonely farmer: Not going out but I am a pilot so I guess that's my hobby

DL Saucy: Really do you fly everywhere for an airline.

Lonely farmer: No just pleasure flying mainly in the west

DL Saucy: oh OK so you never fly into Rochester New York

Lonely farmer: no never never that far sorry

DL Saucy: Oh OK just asking do you get discounts on flying places though ...hey question ...are pilots like backseat drivers when they fly with someone else flying the plane?

Lonely farmer: I don't get any discounts and you are right about backseat drivers

DL Saucy: LOL holy cow I can't imagine not liking the way a pilot flies!

Lonely farmer: Well the one that sits on the left he is a pilot in command so he has the say so

> DL Saucy: AHH but you can't put on the brakes like you can in a car LOL
>
> Lonely farmer: No you can't do that

After confessing that I was not sleeping well Donna invited me to contact her most any time, day or night. "I don't sleep much either," she said.

> Lonely farmer: How late do you stay up
>
> DL Saucy: Sometimes all night like till 4 AM
>
> Lonely farmer: OK if I can't sleep I will write to you

Our chats were casual and candid. We shared more family details, personal history, and dreams, we philosophized a bit, joked, and quite soon after our relationship began I asked a question that had begun to nag at me.

> Lonely farmer: What do your daughters think about you and me writing back-and-forth
>
> DL Saucy: they don't care and even if they did it's too bad it's my life I did my motherly duties and I hope I taught them not to judge people how about yours?
>
> Lonely farmer: I guess i'm a little embarrassed about it because I haven't told them ... all I know is that I love doing this it makes me feel better

Truth is, my chats with Donna were so absorbing and made me so happy, that I began to feel guilty, like I was cheating on my wife. For the first time in fifty years my happiness could not be shared with Shirley.

Eventually, as one hopeful chat led to another, I told my children and extended-family members about Donna. Mostly, everyone was pleased (maybe relieved) that I'd found someone other than my doctor to talk to.

The only wipe-out was one of my wife's nieces who said the new relationship was disrespectful to Shirley and therefore she would never speak to me again. I guess there is at least one extremist in every family, although she did express my worst fear--guilt.

When chatting with Donna, I experienced a state of bliss, but when I signed off I was confused and withdrawn. It got so bad that I didn't know which end was up.

That's when I started seeing a therapist once a week. It was an attempt to unravel my strange dilemma: Somehow, without quite knowing how or exactly when, Donna and I had become close. As a result, it felt as though my devotion was split between two women, one in the present and one in the past. If I had grieved for a year or so before finding Donna, I'm sure I would not have been twisted into knots. But this was happening only days and weeks after losing Shirley.

Even so, what was so wrong about sharing simple details about our lives?

DL Saucy: It's hot hot hot

Lonely farmer: here too maybe around 100 today.

DL Saucy: yikes go swimming.

Lonely farmer: stay inside with AC on. Mornings here are nice outside but afternoons are really hot.

DL Saucy I'll bet. I don't turn the AC on unless I have to. It gives me headaches. just saying hi to you hope your day is going well

Lonely farmer: I went biking with my granddaughter. Good time ... and I went to a grief counselor this morning. First time in my life I ever did anything like that. I think it was worth it she gave me tips on what to avoid and what to expect. Take one cay at a time. Don't look back and try not to look or plan ahead.

DL Saucy: Exactly_ohn one day at a time one minute at a time. I know it's easy to say but try honey and if you feel yourself lost get on here. you may find you will meet a lot of nice people some are really crazy too. Just laugh at them everyone or the Internet has an issue.. kiss kiss.

Calling me "honey" and then adding "kiss kiss" got to me, I must admit; I was moved, even though these early signs of intimacy only heightened my sense of guilt. Looking back, though, I can also see that I was being invited into the future by a sweet person who made no demands of me. She just wanted to help.

Lonely farmer: ... again thanks for your support and friendship.

DL Saucy: i'm pleased to meet you too life is funny people will come in and out of your life for reason hey you said you went to a grief counselor how was it?

Lonely farmer: she gave me a lot of pointers of what to expect you know how to work through The grief. How to deal with reaction from our kids and so forth. She said my kids will be overprotective because they fear losing me. So all in all it was worth my time I have never done anything like this before.

DL Saucy: it's good you did. New life new experiences

2

Donna

Lonely farmer: what plans do you have this evening?

DL Saucy: i'm ready for bed LOL. It's lethal weapon marathon on TV tonight I'm spending the night with Mel Gibson LOL.

Lonely farmer: OK write me if you want or I will write you tomorrow
hugs and kisses.

Laugh Out Loud. If only I could.

The week before John and I met online, I was severely depressed, thinking life was upside down and probably would never be as I had always hoped.

I was sixty-seven-years-old, morbidly obese at three hundred pounds and only five-feet tall. No wonder I needed a wheelchair or walker to move around.

Sure, maybe I'd feel better if I didn't weigh so much. But why bother? Twice, earlier in life, I'd dropped some pounds only to discover I had cancer. Thinning down didn't seem to be the answer.

The first bout of cancer came when I was forty and ended with a single mastectomy. Was I spared? Not quite. At the same time I was diagnosed a couple of girlfriends were afflicted in the same way. I survived, but they didn't. Guilt had haunted me ever since.

The second date with the Big C happened when I was in my fifties. I'd gone back to college, earned a degree, and was enjoying a burgeoning career when uterine cancer took hold. Obviously, I survived that too, but I was forced to accept Social Security disability payments, Medicaid, and food stamps until I turned sixty-five, when I became eligible for straight social security. Welfare had not been part of my plan, yet here I was feeding off the state.

My depression hit new depths after I took a fall and severely injured myself. Now I needed assistance from a healthcare professional who came to my home daily just to help me clean and dress myself.

Stranded at home, I could not help but ponder the events of a life I would describe as "okay" but not particularly wonderful. Coming to terms with it all was difficult, because I believed God had not and was not listening to me.

In truth, none of the set-backs had suddenly happened; my illnesses and depression developed gradually over many years. They were the result, I suppose, of my family environment and the life--an attitude?--I'd allowed myself to settle into.

At the age of twenty-two I became pregnant. I never married because the father of the child didn't want a baby. Basically, he left me standing at the altar with the ultimatum: "It's me or the kid," the term he used to describe my child. I was Catholic. The "kid" won, and Dena has grown up to be a lovely lady.

But that meant I could no longer socialize in the same way, and as a result I thought my friends wouldn't want me around. Fortunately, that wasn't true--they were incredibly supportive. Throughout our troubles, we all discover who our real friends are.

Then when I finally did marry some years later, the man who said "I do" was a nice fellow but not particularly loving, and there was never any passion in the relationship.

I was proud of my achievements and children, yet I had to

admit that I hadn't enjoyed life as I thought I would.

The problem was, I never dared to dream.

I could not afford to, or so I thought. Or maybe I just stopped dreaming because so many youthful visions of grandeur never panned out, and I just could not bear another disappointment.

Through the years I raised my children, but I did not want to burden my parents and brothers because they had their own problems and I didn't want to bother them with mine. I isolated myself, held it all in, even though everything seemed to be falling apart.

Music had always been a great love of mine, and I had fond memories of listening to my entire family sing together as I was growing up. But singing the blues was not my style either, despite my familiarity with the themes: no love, no money, and no social life.

God, help me. I begged Him. *Please, God. Lift me up.* No matter how much I prayed, nothing changed. Although I was not suicidal, I did wake up every morning and wish I was gone. I wondered every day why He didn't just take me.

At the end of my rope, I added my name to a waiting list for public housing--an assisted-living, low-income apartment--where I assumed I would vegetate until my dying day.

Is the darkest hour just before dawn? If so, the wait was too intolerable and dreary for me to believe anymore in a savior or meaningful sunrise.

My computer was my only way out. Sitting in my makeshift bedroom, the only place I could sleep--my lounge chair--I would surf the Net into the wee hours, exploring.

One night, depressed and bored, I decided to search for a "senior" chat room. I was so tired of all those sites designed for young people. I wanted to talk with someone my own age, a person with lots of life experience. I found a platform that looked interesting and opened an account.

That's when it happened. Dawn. God's grace. A man who also

had nothing to live for came calling.

At first it was a simple introduction.

Lonely farmer: I'm a new member ...

After reading his profile, I thought, *I like this guy. He's real and friendly--and oh so sad.*

Like me.

3

Donna

DL Saucy: sorry about last night I had a pretty bad night also did you come online.

Lonely farmer: no I just kept tossing and turning most of the night.

DL Saucy: well I had a pretty tearful night too.

As soon as we began our online chats, JP and I knew they were uplifting, even if they didn't or couldn't entirely cure the sadness we felt about our lives. While JP grappled with a brand-new demon--the enormous empty space created by the death of his wife--I contended with a chronic loneliness that plagued me even when I was in a room full of people.

We both needed each other desperately, yet our relationship was still so young that, at times, we wouldn't seek companionship when we most needed it for fear that one would become a burden to the other.

Lonely farmer: I thought about writing to you but I thought it might bother you.

But what else did I or JP have to do with our long hours of free time?

Pain seems unbeatable when it's experienced alone. The night JP didn't reach out I had logged on at the website. It was about 1 a.m. Eastern Standard Time, which meant it was 10 p.m. in Washington state, many hours to go before dawn would bring some light into my new friend's life. The following day I admitted that I knew how it felt to be lonely and miss someone. This was my way of assuring him there was no need to be shy.

Yet even as I was encouraging JP to contact me any time, I had my own reasons for holding back. I'd already had one online romance, and I'd been jilted. The whole escapade made me feel old and foolish. That I could fall in love with someone a million miles away and loan him money that would never be returned only proved how gullible I could be.

When I confessed this sketchy episode to JP, he was typically patient and understanding.

> Lonely farmer: I don't think you are a fool you can't help who you fall in love with.

His kind response led to me revealing another secret: the cad's name had been John.

> Lonely farmer: oh wow.

> DL Saucy: and what's even funnier is that my ex-husband's name is John too LOL.

> Lonely farmer: wow some coincidence.

I thought I should mention it, because my ex-husband was living in my home at the time, along with my daughter and granddaughter. Other than the name, these other men had nothing in common with my lonely farmer, as far as I could tell. But they took advantage of me, or tried to, and so they all became indicators of my poor track record in matters of the heart.

Not that my ex-husband is a bad person. He's helpful to others; a decent guy. But despite a license on record at the county seat, we never really had a marriage because there was no passion, no spark, no love. It was a sexless union of convenience. He needed a mom for his kids, and I needed a dad for mine. He popped the question one day while we were on a drive.

"How would you like to be married to a dirty old truck driver?"

Thinking I had nothing better to do, and fully aware that I had no intention of ever falling in love again, I said, "Okay."

We would legally separate years later, even though we remained fixtures in each other's lives long after. Pulling away was difficult for me because it felt selfish; I didn't want to hurt him or anybody else. My mentality was a me-against-them proposition. If I was happy, I feared everyone around me would be unhappy. Perhaps I thought I was making an important parental sacrifice by dimming my hopes so that everyone else could get on living their dreams.

Secretly, though, I longed for a normal life with a man I loved and who loved me back. The desire for mutual love consumed me.

I would sit in my oversized recliner chair set in a corner of the living room (my own little piece of the world), stare out the window at the sky and surrender to a day dream . . . or erotic dream:

My love comes home to find me cooking over the stove. He takes the spoon from my hand and bends over to kiss my neck. He presses himself against me and makes me tingle, then he caresses me. His hand covers my one breast. I moan and reach back to massage him until he gets hard. We're now hotter than the sauce bubbling in the pot of the stove. As his hands wander all over my body, I cry out, "God, that feels good, honey. Don't stop. Please don't stop!"

Then I'd snap out of it and return to the real world--the world I hated. That's why chatting with my lonely farmer felt so soothing. I was transported, pulled out of the environment that I found bland and limited.

Even so, there was one thing I needed to change about my online relationship. In an attempt to put some distance between then and now, I asked my new John if he would please allow me to call him JP.

He agreed. Some changes in life come easier than others.

In truth, more was happening to me than I was aware of. It took me days and weeks to realize that a transformation was in progress.

I may have despaired that I was trapped in a body that needed some tender loving care and lots of healing. And I think it is fair to say I was worn out by the financial worries that plague anyone subsisting on a fixed income.

Regardless, the miracle I had desperately prayed for was taking shape and challenging me to reconsider my habitual drift toward negativity.

4

JP

Lonely farmer: when is your birthday?

DL Saucy: June 22nd 1948

Lonely farmer: m ne is March 11, 1943

DL Saucy: five years older

Not that age matters. Why should it--at our age? But maybe I was feeling my years, or my loneliness when I said:

Lonely farmer: it is what it is

DL Saucy: why you say that ... it's good. It is good because we are basically the same age

Lonely farmer: I know thank you for that The older we get the closer our ages are

But I was wishing our bodies were closer. I barely knew Donna, yet so quickly I wanted to reach out and touch her. Like a teenager. And that's funny because that's how our conversation began that day.

Lonely farmer: I just woke up, slept really good maybe because I didn't sleep very good the night before also I took some Z quill. Last night all that talking back-and-forth kind of made me feel like a teenager again. Boy that sounds corny.

DL Saucy: morning John. We are teenagers in our minds.

Lonely farmer: well I suppose so. Did you just wake up?

DL Saucy: NO NO....No supposing. it can be true inside Our minds. It can be true. Yes I just woke.

Lonely farmer: wow me too about 10 minutes.

DL Saucy: we're on the same cycle.

She would challenge certain mental concepts or assumptions. The kind of things "old folks" can fall into. I liked that because I realized it wasn't just having somebody to talk to that was pulling me out of my grief, it was the new ideas, the feisty insistence that Donna brought to our chats.

And if I got out of bed at odd hours just to fit into her day, I didn't mind. As I explained to Donna, when I stay in bed more than five hours my back starts to hurt and I have to get up anyway. Why not get up and talk with a beautiful lady?

Lonely farmer: What kinds of things do you have planned today? Are you still there? I told you the other day that I was kind of embarrassed to tell my kids that we are talking back-and-forth. Well I told a couple of them yesterday and they thought it was great!!! Not that I need or want their approval.

> DL Saucy: yeah I know what you mean are they used to seeing you on the computer?
>
> Lonely farmer: Or a desktop yes but not like this on a cell phone.

As we learned about each other's maladies and daily routines (Donna had taken a fall that had harmed some tendons, muscles, and nerves, and all that took longer to heal than a broken bone), we also began to confess a kind of separation anxiety. Crazy. As the song goes, "We've Only Just Begun."

> DL Saucy: Did you have coffee yet?
>
> Lonely farmer: no not yet. How about you? I usually get up and take a shower then coffee and I'm about ready to.
>
> DL Saucy: Nope ... usually have my breakfast first then shower.
>
> Lonely farmer: I didn't want to leave you!
>
> DL Saucy: Me too I know.... LOL.... well let's go do our morning stuff then will come back whenever we can.
>
> Lonely farmer: OK I will talk to you later
>
> DL Saucy: we can talk back-and-forth if you are here answer... if not ...well. if not well so be it. we can answer each other later and sooner or later we will be here together at the same time OK?
>
> Lonely farmer: I'm still here.
>
> DL Saucy: Lol me too

Lonely farmer: OK

DL Saucy: Unless of course you want to take the phone with you to the shower and talk to me...LOL...just kidding go.... I'll TTYL (talk to you later)

Lonely farmer: Okay I am Going.

DL Saucy: Kiss kiss Hug Hug

That was another thing about Donna that I enjoyed. She was affectionate. Her digital hugs and kisses were dear to me. Another person might not want to be so thoughtful or tender so soon. But we felt a tug, an immediacy every time we communicated.

She also was a good teacher. I soon got the hang of the online short-hand, which was a big help, especially when I was texting on my cellphone.

TTYL (talk to you later)

OMG (oh my god!)

LOL (laugh out loud)

BRB (be right back)

IDK (I don't know)

WB (welcome back)

"and if you need a hug well XXXXXXXXX is for hugs and if you need a kiss OOOOOOOO IS FOR kisses so XOXOXOX means hugs and kisses."

That last tip came in one of our earliest talks, when she was preparing to sign off so that she could spend the night with Mel Gibson movies featured in an all-night marathon.

> Lonely farmer: well you better watch your movie XOXOXOX
>
> DL Saucy: no 'm here with you unless you're tired
>
> Lonely farmer: I'm OK so I'm here with you
>
> DL Saucy: John if were there I would give you a hug and kiss you

That fired me up, for sure. It was a foreshadowing of Las Vegas (though we had yet to discuss that possibility) and an indicator of how fast we were moving toward an intimacy that I guess would be compared to phone sex.

But two people of our generation don't just fall into bed without a courtship. Or do they?

Donna and I could be having a simple conversation about our children and family life when suddenly it would hit me: Life is too short. What are we waiting for? If not now, when?

> DL Saucy: When your second daughter leaves will you be alone?
>
> Lonely farmer: no someone will be with me.
>
> DL Saucy: Ahh always? That's great. My daughter And my granddaughter live upstairs from me. But my granddaughter is leaving for college next week.
>
> Lonely farmer: Enjoy her before she leaves. Where does

she go to college and what is she taking?

DL Saucy: DNA forensics. She goes to Brockport state. The school is only about 40 minutes away. But she's going to live on campus. First time away from home. Boo-hoo.

Lonely farmer: Is she a freshman?

DL Saucy: Third year she's going into her third year she took her first two years at home at Monroe Community College.

Lonely farmer: I know it seems like they grow up so fast.

If Donna and I were experiencing a second adolescence, we both knew that it might not last as long as the first. Seize the day. Seize every minute. Express raw truths, naked truths, because there was no more time or need for regrets and might-have-beens.

DL Saucy: so you were asking about Ballroom dancing do you like to dance

Lonely farmer: yes I always wanted to take lessons but never did

DL Saucy: Ahhhh well I could teach you

Lonely farmer: I was never very good at it I'll bet you're good at it

DL Saucy: well I was when I was better

Lonely farmer: well as they say nothing lasts forever we can't stay young forever

DL Saucy: I know and I hate it

Lonely farmer: Me too

DL Saucy: I hate it so let's stay young forever

Lonely farmer: OK I'm all for it

DL Saucy: good then come on let's go dancing right now

Lonely farmer: OK how we going to do that? I think of my younger years but it's not Enough. I want more

DL Saucy: I want more too I want more I'm not ready to give up being young

Lonely farmer: I know

DL Saucy: LOL

Lonely farmer: life is all too short

DL Saucy: c'est la vie I know

Lonely farmer: I heard a joke yesterday life is like a roll of toilet paper the closer you get to end the faster it goes

DL Saucy: LOL LCL LOL

Lonely farmer: Donna it's almost 11:30 PM there you better get some sleep

DL Saucy: it's so true about life. I know we should say good night John. you don't want to do you?

Lonely farmer: this has been fun I hope we can continue tomorrow

DL Saucy: OK good night sleep well I'm going to finish the dishes and go to sleep kiss kiss night John

Lonely farmer: OK good night I'll talk to you in the night or early morning

DL Saucy: okey-dokey

Lonely farmer: kiss kisses to you

DL Saucy: night donna

Lonely farmer: Nite

I hated that word: goodnight.

5

Donna/JP

Lonely farmer: right back at you kisses too. Donna I'm home
now if you want to talk. It may sound kind of weird but as I
was gone most of the day I kept looking at my phone to see
if you wrote me I think I'm hooked on talking to you.

Hi Donna I missing you where are you I miss seeing you
hello Donna where are you I'm missing you are you OK talk
to me hello

DL Saucy: hi I just got home HI there.

I was thrilled to find JP's text, which included his earlier attempts
to reach me. I know my kids love me. My brothers, too. And I have
a few good friends. Now, a man on the other side of the world was
showing that he was capable of those loving feelings. To be needed
. . . that's love, right?

The whole thing, the sudden attachment reminded me of a
song. The chorus starts with, "I . . . I'm hooked on a feeling." That's
what it was. Hooked on the feeling of togetherness, though we
were thousands of miles apart.

Lonely farmer: hi did you read my earlier message because
I really meant it seems kind of crazy for an old guy to feel

this way but I really think I'm hooked on talking to you.

DL Saucy: hi give me a sec I'm going to check my balance in my checking account.... that's so nice honey really... that you feel that way I think I'm hooked also on talking to you too

Donna would affirm my feelings and share hers whenever I admitted what I was really experiencing. I don't know that I'd ever quite had that same experience with a woman. When we're young we play around a bit, not wanting to give our heart too soon, not wanting to be embarrassed.

But within a few days we were admitting that we needed this connectivity on a regular basis. We had no reason to pretend otherwise.

I began to realize it even affected whether or not we accepted invitations or went out to do simple chores.

Lonely farmer: so is your balance OK sorry none of my business

DL Saucy: LOL just a sec I haven't even logged on yet

Lonely farmer: OK

DL Saucy: what are you doing

Lonely farmer: just sitting down here waiting for you to write

DL Saucy: OK $5.28 in my checking account LOL

Lonely farmer: I don't think that's enough!

DL Saucy: LOL it's enough for a nice cap at Tim Hortons

Lonely farmer: just barely

DL Saucy: LOL

Lonely farmer: what are you doing now

DL Saucy: tomorrow is payday

Lonely farmer: oh good

DL Saucy: I was just talking to my brother he's in a band he wants to know if I want to go see him play I was thinking about it but I'm not sure how much energy I have

Lonely farmer: OK if you want we can talk another time or later but I will miss you

DL Saucy: if I go it won't be for at least one hour and a half want to come with me?

Lonely farmer: I would like to

DL Saucy: LOL OK will pick you up

Lonely farmer: Ok what kind of band

DL Saucy: he has a two-piece duo ... he plays guitar and sings ...his partner has all the technology Instruments that give you all the background music. They do a lot of 60s and 70s and Frank Sinatra stuff like that

Lonely farmer: oh I think I would like that

DL Saucy: oh fine ots of fun

Lonely farmer: what time do you have to leave

DL Saucy: 9:30 PM if I go I'm kind of tired and I'm not one for loud music

Lonely farmer: me either must be an age thing what time would you get back

DL Saucy: 11 it's right up the road where he's playing very close to home I don't usually go but now he's so close it may be OK for me to go

Lonely farmer: maybe you should go you might have fun

DL Saucy: but like I said IDK...that means I don't know... i've been there and done that ...I don't want to spend the night with a bunch of drunks. Although it is an older crowd LOL my age and people can't afford to buy drinks out anymore

Lonely farmer: I wouldn't like being around drunks either

DL Saucy: I know

Lonely farmer: by the way do you drink if at all I have about two glasses of wine a year that's all I'm sorry I should'nt have asked that

DL Saucy: of course you can ask me

Lonely farmer: well I don't want to be pushy I really enjoy talking to you

DL Saucy: I don't drink much and occasional margarita or glass of wine and on a really hot day I may have a beer

Lonely farmer: I forgot I like a margarita once in a while like once a year ...a frozen margarita.

DL Saucy: Yep it's so good frozen

Lonely farmer: I know I wish I could buy you one

DL Saucy: MMMM it would be good tonight

Lonely farmer: I know

DL Saucy: what did you used to do for fun.

Lonely farmer: I can't believe I'm doing this I mean glued to my phone waiting to hear from you! I used to go to Reno Nevada and play poker machines and sometimes blackjack

JP was so open and kind I didn't want to share him. I encouraged him to seek other people online. It seemed like the fair thing to do: The more the merrier.

Maybe he would be better off gambling in Reno. We were realizing why the younger generations spend so much time online with computers and their phones. It's addictive.

DL Saucy: it's something new and easy to get hooked on. You should meet lots of people on here you can be fun

Lonely farmer: why do I need to be with more people?

DL Saucy: it's fun

Lonely farm: OK

DL Saucy: it's interesting I mean you don't have to

Please don't stray, is what I was really thinking. When the flame is lit you don't want it to fade. And I had quickly warmed to the idea of having a constant companion, though I didn't dare believe it could happen, or know how it might work out, nor did I want to *expect* it to happen. That sounded like another opportunity for disappointment.

Yet . . . yet this felt like destiny.

DL Saucy: have you ever talked to another woman on here

Lonely farmer: once a couple days ago but I got bored. you are everything but boring

DL Saucy: what was different about her

Lonely farmer: well she seemed very religious and I'm not very so I got kind of bored are you very religious sorry again none of my business I don't want to do anything to ruin our fun

DL Saucy: well I believe there's a higher power call it whatever you want call it God Buddha Messiah Allah the force it doesn't matter I am a Catholic I do Believe that people come into our life for a reason but no I'm not a religious fanatic I go to church occasionally my brother left our Catholic Church and now he belongs to a non-denominational church

Lonely farmer: I think you have a good point I sort of believe the same I also go to church occasionally very occasionally

DL Saucy: my relationship with that power I'll call him God is between me and God, he's the only one that knows my heart for real

Donna was so generous that I might have explored our online platform a bit more--if I hadn't already found Donna, the woman I enjoyed being with.

At the same time, I could not presume she didn't have other relationships that interested her. So I tip-toed gently into those waters.

Lonely farmer: do you have more friends ?

DL Saucy: yeah, a few

Lonely farmer: OK that's cool

DL Saucy: my kids my brothers my girlfriends and yes men friends too I was hooked on someone online

Lonely farmer: was it good or what

DL Saucy: well I actually met him one time when he was here visiting my cousin and he was with her so I didn't really think anything of it

Lonely farmer: I've never been online with anyone before. You're the first and it's great

DL Saucy: he was here for three days we had fun my cousin and me and him but my cousin died and I had to tell him and then we kind a got close because of that but he's not into it like he was in the beginning because maybe one or two times a month kind of broke my heart

The man was Scottish. He flew to the Rochester area to meet my cousin Sarah, who asked me to be her chaperone and help break the ice. When we were introduced, he said "Hello, Donna" with the sweetest brogue. Even when uttering simple words he created sounds that were among the most beautiful I'd ever heard. And when he shook my hand I savored the masculine tactile sensation.

The next day we spoke in his hotel lobby for about an hour before Sarah arrived for their day of fun. I could tell that John and I--yes, another John--were hitting it off, especially when he kissed me on the cheek and gave me a hug when my cousin finally arrived. Oh, how I savored the nearness of a charming man. But I had to keep my feelings in check. This was Sarah's new boyfriend, not mine.

After John returned to Scotland, the three of us would occasionally chat online. So when Sarah died suddenly it was me who had to break the sad news. The more we spoke, the more we confessed our mutual attraction the time he visited America. I thought we were in love.

As the relationship grew, I occasionally asked if he might want to make a return trip to Rochester. Yet when I did, he seemed to retreat, so I didn't push. Then his behavior turned erratic. In mid-conversation he'd say "I'll be right back" and then leave me waiting, never to return. The next time we hooked up online, he'd have all kinds of excuses, like his computer had crashed (that's handy) or he'd had an emergency.

John the Scotsman was likely talking to other women online, though I was in denial for a while. Eventually, it began to erode my self-esteem. Heck, what was it that I lacked that Sarah had had? John would fly across the ocean to visit her, but not me.

Even online a woman has to have some pride, right? LOL. So after he'd left me hanging one too many times, I decided *I'm done with this jerk*. Never heard from him again.

Another online Romeo showed his true colors real quick into the so-called relationship. He loved me, oh boy did he sweet talk me, and even sent flowers, though he hailed from a third-world country.

Then he requested my bank account number.

Darling, why so ever would you need that kind of info?

He claimed to have an astronomical amount of money he needed to deposit in my American account so that he could visit me stateside. Uh huh.

I strung him along just to see what else he might lie about. Then I researched online scams. Bingo! There he was. Hey, I may be dumb but I'm not stupid. Sayonara, Boy Toy.

So there I was, "Alone again, naturally." There is a good song for every kind of heartbreak.

Lonely farmer: like I told you yesterday I feel kind a like a teenager talking to you

DL Saucy: it's fun

Lonely farmer: yes it is

DL Saucy: just be careful guard your heart I like you a lot

Lonely farmer: it's taking my mind off of other things me too I kind a like you too we seem to kind of connect

DL Saucy: I know but that's easy to do here online

Lonely farmer: I suppose so

DL Saucy: typing and reading this gets into your head. it consumes you

Lonely farmer: you're so right

DL Saucy: so here's a fake big big big big hug XXXXXXX

Lonely farmer: thanks for the big hug

DL Saucy: MMMMMMM MEANS MMMMMMM LOL

Lonely farmer: I forgot what does X mean

DL Saucy: hug silly O means kiss

Lonely farmer: OK then XXXXXXXX

DL Saucy: XOXOXOX

Lonely farmer: oh XOXOX

6

Donna/JP

Lonely farmer: It's 12 o'clock your time and I'm still awake if you want to talk.

DL Saucy: hi

Lonely farmer: it's three AM my time I'm going to try to sleep a little more and you?

It's about 5 AM my time I'm going to get up and shower unless you're awake and want to talk

Amazingly, it had only been a few days since I'd gone online and met Donna, but already I wanted to be with her more and more. She was fun to be with and eased the ever present, aching loneliness inside. I still loved my wife, and always would. We'd shared a life and a family together, and she'd loved me too. But Donna helped fill the hole her love left. I wasn't replacing Shirley, so much as finding someone new to talk to. Someone I just couldn't get enough of.

When I woke, whether it was with the dawn or much earlier because I couldn't sleep, I thought of Donna. She'd told me it was okay to message her anytime, so I did. Midnight, three o'clock in the morning, six a.m. with the birds. I just wanted to be with her, and she was always friendly in return. I worried that I'd push her away, that I was too needy wanting to be in contact all the time.

But she was just Donna, happy, laughing, supportive, but with a depth of pain inside that made me want to protect her, take care of her. I knew she was fine without me, but that didn't stop me from wanting to help her.

Each day I wanted to know more and more about her. I realized I wanted to know everything about her. But how far would she let me in?

> Lonely farmer: I was wondering how tall you are I'm 6'3" 215 pounds
>
> DL Saucy: Here's my pic honey this is me. 5 foot not skinny red hair
>
> Lonely farmer: I can take a selfie of me but I don't know how to send it
>
> DL Saucy: hit the camera Icon take the picture then you just hit the green arrow to the right.
>
> Lonely farmer: Your beautiful!!!! You have beautiful red hair!! Why don't you give me your email address and I can send you my picture
>
> DL Saucy: let's wait a bit

That same day we began sharing pictures of ourselves, and Donna was beautiful on the outside too. I could tell she was worried about her weight and maybe what I thought of her looks. But I knew what she had in her heart, and she could have had three eyes and a horn for all I cared. But she didn't. She had beautiful red hair, to match her sparkly personality, and a wonderful smile. Everything I learned about her just made me want to get closer.

The technology kept tripping me up, but she was so patient. She never seemed to get angry or impatient even though I was all thumbs sometimes. Later I realized that she was allowing me to be whoever I was, without any judgment.

DL Saucy: very nice very handsome see you got the hang of it

Lonely farmer: donna you have made my day. You told me you were 67. How come you look much younger you are beautiful.

DL Saucy: LOL yeah...but you need glasses!!!

Lonely farmer: I have glasses I mean it you're beautiful

DL Saucy: well maybe you need new glasses ha ha but thank you

Lonely farmer: kind of Mushy

DL Saucy: Yep LOL it's OK though you're allowed

Lonely farmer: OK. I haven't had this much fun for a long time I wish you could teach me ballroom dancing.

DL Saucy: but please take it easy Ray. I don't want to be the person that breaks your heart. I have a lot of issues going on right now in my life for instance an ex who hangs around all the time LOL

Lonely farmer: did you call me ray?

DL Saucy: lol spellchecker puts its own words in sometime.
All my men are named John. Lol seriously.

Lonely farmer: I would not want to break your heart either.
I think yours has been broken enough

DL Saucy: my life sucks over here I know that's the other
thing.
I don't want to happen to you what happens to me. I fall
hard and fast

Lonely farmer: I hope it won't

DL Saucy: and very deeply I'm beginning to like you a lot

Lonely farmer: me too and I'm not just saying that I mean it

I was afraid to show JP a picture of me. After all, I was very overweight and only five feet tall! What if it turned him off? It wasn't like I was twenty and curvy anymore. But he didn't seem to mind a bit; he even called me beautiful. The man needed glasses!

I worried that maybe he was falling too fast. And that I was too. So I kept pushing him away, a little bit. I mean, I didn't want him to go away at all, but I was afraid of what would happen if I let him have my heart. Every time before, for all my life, I'd been hurt by my heart. I didn't want it to happen again, but what could I do if I kept liking him more and more?

I also worried that he was falling for me too fast. He'd only lost his wife three weeks earlier. Was it really possible to fall in love with someone else so soon? Was he crazy? Was I crazy?

Either way, we talked all the time. Or texted, whatever it was called. And we shared more and more and more.

Lonely farmer: what more if anything do you want to know about me

DL Saucy: was your marriage a good one do you mind talking about it?

Lonely farmer: It was a great one we never fought and no I don't mind talking about it what else would you like to know

DL Saucy: just that for now

Lonely farmer: we are both easy-going and worked side-by-side on our farm

I'm pretty sure JP would have told me anything I asked him. It seemed like he wanted to, he wanted to share his life with me. He'd had a wonderful marriage, but I wasn't jealous of it. Instead, I wondered if maybe we'd been together too, kind of at the same time but apart. Like God wanted us to know each other, but was saving us for being together later.

And then I wondered if I was just being a silly kid, because that's what it was like with him. We could talk about anything, and we could play too.

DL Saucy: my other daughter and her children live upstairs from my mom and dad. We take care of mom and dad 92 and 87 years old. we all do our part to make sure they're comfortable. I just took my shower and I'm doing my hair as I talk to you

Lonely farmer: Boy that's so nice of you to still have parents alive even if they are declining

DL Saucy: I know and they have helped all of us 1 million times over

Lonely farmer: oh that's great!!! how do you do your hair and type at the same time

DL Saucy: it is great...I have a great family ...LOL... I curl and hold and type...curl and hold and type...curl and hold and type.lol

Lonely farmer: how long does it take to do your hair you must be good at it being an ex hairdresser

DL Saucy: yes I can do it with my eyes closed it takes me sometimes 10 minutes
sometimes longer depending on what I'm doing

I worried sometimes that Donna would get tired of me, bored with this old farmer too far out west. Especially when I found out she'd returned to college when she was fifty-years-old and got three degrees! I'd never been to college and only had degrees in greasy truck engines and busted irrigation pipes. But hers were in the science of disability disciplines with an emphasis in psychology. Holy cow. She used her college training to advise disabled people on how to return to the work force. The more I knew her, the more impressed I was.

What did she want with an old farmer like me? It kept me awake sometimes. She was smart and beautiful and had a life and family back east. I just had to hope the higher powers had something in mind for us, because I was smitten. From head to toe. The most I could do was just tell her how wonderful she was and how much I cared. No matter what had happened in her life or what her circumstances were now, I would understand. I had to. She was the one thing in life that brought me happiness.

Also, I knew that Donna had a lot going on in her life, and it all showed what a good heart she had. Her parents were still alive, and she spent a lot of time looking after them. So even though she'd had bad luck with men, I realized her family was important for her. It was for me too, so I understood that. We had those old time values in common. I mean, both her and her children helped look after her parents, so she must have been a good mother too.

But what really got to me was her playfulness. She could turn any old thing into something fun, and how many people can say that? It was a constant adventure with her, and she was always teaching me something. It wasn't just that I was filling the hole the death of my wife left. Donna helped with my loneliness, sure. I wasn't sitting around wondering what to do with my time. But it was more than that. Even though I'd been happy with my life, Donna filled a part that had been overlooked. She made me laugh and see the wonder in small things.

In other words, she made me happy like I had never been happy before.

I tried to reassure her that I was for real. I didn't want her thinking that I was another person who would hurt her. At the same time, I didn't want to move too fast. I knew she was cautious, that she was attracted to me, but also wary. If she would just let me in I would prove to her I was different.

> DL Saucy: those little planes scare me. I was on a 12 seater once and I didn't like it

> Lonely farmer: I know but you have to be careful and avoid weather problems

DL Saucy: yeah i don't even remember why I didn't like it

Lonely farmer: I have been flying for 41 years so I kinda know what to avoid.

DL Saucy: I'm sure

Lonely farmer: I would imagine that the this online talking website is full of BS but I can assure you that I am not full of BS. I have done very well financially so rest assured no BS FROM ME
I love your picture. I put it on my lock screen.

DL Saucy: awww

I knew right off that JP was a family person. Most of his children were from his wife's first marriage, but I knew it didn't matter to him. He loved them like they were his own.

He was caring and talented--he could fly one of those little planes!--and he seemed to be different from the other men I'd known. So even though I was afraid at times, I tiptoed in deeper. He couldn't be all bad, could he? I mean, he wouldn't lead me astray, right?

DL Saucy: we love our kids but omg those grandchildren are so special and wonderful

Lonely farmer: I agree. That's why it hurt so much when my granddaughter Jennifer came down with Leukemia right after a vacation. And now she's taking chemo in Seattle

DL Saucy: yuk

Lonely farmer: She is doing ok and has about 3 more months of treatment.

DL Saucy: that's the worst ..but I hear they have come a long way with chemo

I was learning we had the same values. That was a relief! And we also loved a lot of the same things, like music. I'd been raised in a musical family. My parents loved music and they instilled that love in my brothers and me. So I listened to everything, from Barbara Streisand to Shania Twain to even a little bit of rap every now and then. JP loved music too, from 50s and 60s rock--love that stuff--to country to Lawrence Welk. You couldn't ask for more.

We chatted all the time now, so we were able to get to know all kinds of things about each other. Not like what people do today, where you go out on dates and hook up and God knew what happened early on. We'd only known each other a few days, but we talked about everything it seemed. And if there was anything I wanted to know I just had to ask. Or he'd bring it up seeming to know what I wanted to know.

Lonely farmer: I don't want to bore you

DL Saucy: my tummy hurts a little
oh stop your not boring me

Lonely farmer: You probably didn't get enough sleep last night

DL Saucy: I'm just old lol

Lonely farmer: Can't help you with your tummy

DL Saucy: I slept about 6 hours, I think

Lonely farmer: If you think you're old what about me

DL Saucy: Your ok your young

Lonely farmer: Ha ha you the one who needs new glasses

DL Saucy: lololololol

He was so sweet worrying about boring me. If only he knew it was the opposite. I couldn't wait to see his messages. I found myself waking up at night checking for him, looking to see if he was awake too, and many times he was.

Where was this relationship going? I didn't want to think about it, but yet I did anyway. I was having fun, for the first time in forever, and didn't want it to stop--ever.

But my previous online relationships had ended in heartbreak, so would this one too? It was just that JP seemed so different. He seemed to care about people. People he loved. And he'd done so many amazing things.

Even so, I worried about him too. His wife had just died, so what kind of state could he be in? Maybe I was just his rebound, or whatever it was called. Maybe I was just there to help him through this and he would go.

So I needed to push him away sometimes, just to protect myself. Well, and him too. This was going so fast it was kind of crazy. Would we spin out of control and crash into each other?

Lonely farmer: One of my cars is a Corvette and the other is a classic 1955 Chevy

DL Saucy: wow
In 1955 I was 7 years old

Lonely farmer: I know and I was 12

DL Saucy: Yesterday

Lonely farmer: One I traded in on a new Camero for my Granddaughter that has leukemia

DL Saucy: awwww what a nice grandpa

Lonely farmer: Well she really wanted one and I thought it would help her get through it

DL Saucy: awesome

Lonely farmer: You want to go for a ride and listen to the radio?

DL Saucy: oh yes

Lonely farmer: I'll pick you up

DL Saucy: k

Lonely farmer: Be right there

DL Saucy: Ha ha

DL Saucy: blast the music

Lonely farmer: It would be fun though wouldn't it

DL Saucy: sure would

Lonely farmer: Bring back old memories

DL Saucy: mm it does

7

Donna/JP

Lonely farmer: I just want to put my arms around you

DL Saucy: Watch out for emotions, they will creep up on
you
And you'll be lost in space and time in a different
dimension ...THE TWILIGHT ZONE HA HA

We got more and more relaxed together. It was as if Donna and I
really were sitting next to each other. We felt what each other was
feeling, and more importantly, we cared. It was as if we were living
together already. Well, almost. We could pretend most anything,
and immediately it was as if we were there doing it. Driving her to
church in one of my cars, her smiling and laughing all the way, or us
teasing or being silly.

I thought of her all the time, and wondered what she was
doing, what she was thinking. When I asked she always told me,
and she always made me feel good. I couldn't get close enough
to her, I couldn't get enough. My loneliness was still there, and
I still missed Shirley, her memory was sacred, and always would
be. But Donna allowed the good feelings to come back, a place for
happiness. I hoped I did that for her too.

Lonely farmer: Okay I'm trying to watch my emotions but.....
It's like you are finding a way in my heart
And I like it
Sorry
Mushy

DL Saucy: Ohhh boy ...please be careful john. We can have all kinds of fun but please be careful with those, emotions, right now. You are in a very fragile state of mind.
I can be here for u
But that's all I can do right now

Lonely farmer: I know
Thanks I will try

DL Saucy: U can close your eyes
And imagine if u will
that I am right there in front of you and you put your arms around me
And I'll give you the warmest hug u ever had

Lonely farmer: Oh boy, I wish you were here

DL Saucy: mmm I am, in spirit

Lonely farmer: What a great hug

DL Saucy: and even if u like a kiss
a soft gentle warm kiss

Lonely farmer: How about 2 kisses

DL Saucy: 2 it is
do I hear 3?

Lonely farmer: Oh yes
And more hugs

DL Saucy: going, once
going twice
sold
to the guy in the 1955 blue Chevy

I wanted Donna to know about me too, to know about my life, the good and the bad. I wanted to make sure she was okay with who I was. I guess I was protecting myself. If she didn't like something about me now, then she wouldn't be surprised when we met, if we ever met. I still didn't know how that would work out.

So I told her about me physically, how seven years ago I had a fibrillation in my heart. Then three years ago I'd been diagnosed with bladder cancer, and they thought it was because I used to smoke. The cancer was okay now, but I had a bad back too. I knew she had health issues, bigger ones than I did, but I wanted her to know we all had something wrong with us physically--especially as we got older. I wanted her to know it was safe to tell me anything she wanted to. That I would accept her for who she was. I knew her heart was good and that's all that really mattered, although I found her physically attractive too.

She told me about her physical ailments, and she had a lot. I knew she was suffering, and I didn't want her to. It was amazing how we could talk about the most private, deepest aspects of ourselves and our lives, and then switch to discussing Family Feud. All like it was the most natural thing in the world. There were no limits, it was all kind and supportive and fun.

JP wanted to talk about our physical problems, so I told him. Might as well get it out.

> DL Saucy: I have battled depression all my life. I have a chemical imbalance.. I get panic attacks ..I have a hernia that is wrapping around my bowel. ..u know about the arthritis. ..and the cancer. I have neuropathy in my foot, shall I go on..lol
> oh yeah and I am over weight
> I have a doctor for every part of my body, lol

Amazingly, he didn't mind. The more I told him about me, the more he seemed to like me. He was the absolute opposite of every man I had ever had a relationship with.

> Lonely farmer: This is the part of getting old that really sucks
>
> DL Saucy: I'm ok though john. Really i deal with things
>
> Lonely farmer: We all have something

I could tell JP was getting bitten hard by the love bug, and truthfully I loved being chased. I loved being appreciated for who I was, even though I wasn't as physically attractive anymore. We were building the friendship, understanding, and respect before all the rest. Through this online thing, we were able to get to know each other even though we lived on opposite sides of the country. We never could have done that years ago, when we were younger.

> DL Saucy: I don't think I'll last all night tonight John

Lonely farmer: Xoxoxo
I know you're tired

DL Saucy: Awww tks
I'm very relaxed, this is very relaxing

Lonely farmer: Did I do the xoxoxo right

DL Saucy: yes perfect

Lonely farmer: If you go to sleep make sure you send me
a message if you wake up early

DL Saucy: U got t

Lonely farmer: I'm trying to be careful

DL Saucy: I know u are

Lonely farmer: But I like you a lot
What can I do

DL Saucy: Ohh boy you got bit
I like u too

Lonely farmer: You re the one that bit me
It's your fault

DL Saucy: But like I said I have issues here

My ex-husband lived in the same house I did, even though we had
nothing to do with each other and hadn't for years. But it must have
seemed strange to JP, so I just explained it to him and hoped he
would understand. Which he did. He was that kind of guy. And

my parents were old and took a lot of time. My dad, especially, was ill. He was in a wheelchair and we all took turns helping my mom out. My granddaughter Gabby was going off to college, and Bonnie was thinking she wanted her own place. She couldn't afford it but didn't know that yet. This with all my physical issues meant my life was complex. And JP took all that away. With him I was happy and having fun, even if he was falling too fast.

> Lonely farmer: I am lonely and you are helping me
>
> DL Saucy: I'm here for you john. I get lonely in a room full of people
>
> Lonely farmer: I know the feeling
> It's nice to talk with somebody that's about my age
> It means a lot

JP always told me nice things about myself. He knew I was a good person, and so I felt safe telling him about me. It wasn't like he was judging me or anything. He just excepted who I was and liked me. I even told him how once I stole some towels from a hotel room. And a flower arrangement too. I guess when someone knows your heart, they don't mind your sins. Or they understand them at least. Later, this was part of why I knew JP and I were meant to be together. God wouldn't let someone who truly knew me, judge against me. Would He?

> DL Saucy: My ship came in, unfortunately it was the titanic lol
>
> Lonely farmer: There's still time
>
> DL Saucy: I have all that I need
> I don't want things anymore like I used to

Lonely farmer: Donna things aren't that bad
Don't give up hope
You deserve more

DL Saucy: Life is too short for wanting material stuff

Lonely farmer: You are a good person

DL Saucy: I try

Lonely farmer: I know
Correction I think you are a great person
I have talked to you enough to know that

Every time I thought we'd gone deep, I found we could go deeper, and still have fun while we did it. We talked about our physical problems and our families and our loneliness, and then Donna would turn around and make a joke and it made us both feel comfortable. It was like explaining who we were allowed us to joke and have fun. Two old people with nothing left to hide, nothing to prove like younger people tried to do. We'd been through all that and come out on the other side.

DL Saucy: and there's one other thing I'm gonna tell you,

Lonely farmer: Ok go ahead I'm sitting down

DL Saucy: I wear depends, lol
ROFLMAO. .anc that means rolling on the floor laughing

my *** off

Lonely farmer: Okay. Do you have a leaking bladder?

DL Saucy: YUP
and they can't operate

Lonely farmer: Are you kidding me?

DL Saucy: cause I have that hernia
no I'm not kidding

Lonely farmer: Well we are getting all the health issues
out in the open

DL Saucy: hell yea
oh and one more thing

Lonely farmer: Okay

DL Saucy: I'm pregnant
and it's yours

Donna could tell me the craziest personal details of her life, and then make me laugh. Over the hours we learned more about each other, and it was all good. No matter how bad it was.

Lonely farmer: It's probably not my baby because my
lower body parts don't work like they used to if at all

DL Saucy: lol
Lonely farmer: We are a mess

DL Saucy: hey I have more fun talking about it then I ever had doing it

Lonely farmer: But the emotions are still working ok and both our hearts can still love and also be broken

Donna became the best part of my day; the only part of my day that I truly looked forward to. And I could tell she felt that way too. We simply didn't want to not be together. All day we checked in with each other, and we stayed awake as long as we could at night so we didn't miss a thing, just like a couple of kids at a slumber party.

One evening she went to where her brother's band was playing, and I stayed up waiting for her to return home, just like I would have if she was my wife. Or girlfriend even. Although it had been so long since I'd had a girlfriend or dated that I wasn't sure what the rules were. I wasn't sure where we were.

But what I did know was that I wanted to talk to Donna even when she wasn't at home. I didn't want to bother her, but I wanted to be able to check in. And if she ever needed anything she could always call me. The problem was, she wouldn't give me her phone number. We tried Yahoo messenger and skype, but often we couldn't make those work right. I let it go for the time and gave Donna her space, but a plan began to hatch for how to talk to her anywhere.

Before long, things began to get . . . physical. Well, as physical as you can get when you're over 2,500 miles apart. It was a little scary at first, I mean we were online! What would my daughter think? But it seemed so natural too. We'd created a safe place between us, and I felt comfortable with John. Besides, if you tell someone you wear Depends, you've got to trust them.

Lonely farmer: Do you feel my arms around you

DL Saucy: yes wait

Lonely farmer: My eyes are open
And I have to wear my glasses to see

DL Saucy: we only had one kiss ..oh I mean 3...how the
hell did u get me in bed already

Lonely farmer: I am a fast worker

DL Saucy: lol

Lonely farmer: I thought it was your idea

DL Saucy: Get that grin off your face

Lonely farmer: Seemed like a good idea

DL Saucy: my idea?

Lonely farmer: You are making me laugh

I was nervous, but I would joke around whenever it got too serious. And JP was always ready to laugh, even when I pushed him away, or brought him in closer, or pushed him away. It was like I didn't know which way to go, except closer, which scared me.

So I joked instead.

Lonely farmer: I think you had too many margaritas
DL Saucy: you said u can't get pregnant from kissing

Lonely farmer: This is more fun than actually doing it I

think. I can't remember though
Been a long time

DL Saucy: so what are you wearing?

Lonely farmer: I always sleep in a tee shirt and underwear

DL Saucy: boxers or briefs

Lonely farmer: Briefs
Boy are you getting personal. I don't mind

DL Saucy: White?
ask me what I'm wearing

Lonely farmer: No it's okay. At my age it's quite a
complement that you would ask. Yes white.
Ok what are you wearing?

DL Saucy: Depends
lol

We had so much fun together, and we were spending most of the day messaging and thinking about each other, how would we ever meet? Maybe we didn't need to. Could you have a relationship just like this? This good but without anything more? I didn't see how else it could end. I had commitments here. My parents weren't well, my dad especially. And my daughters and granddaughters and the rest of my family were here. Well, it was fun being with JP. He made me feel good and safe and loved for the first time in so long.

Lonely farmer: How long have we been doing this
tonight?

DL Saucy: what talking?
I got home around 7 my time, so 5 hours

Lonely farmer: When are you going to sleep

DL Saucy: as soon as you tuck me in

Lonely farmer: Ok I'm tucking you in and giving you a big huge hug.
Can you feel my arms around you?

DL Saucy: mmmm ok and I'm hugging u back

Lonely farmer: Kiss kiss kiss

DL Saucy: ooooooo 3 more
nice

Lonely farmer: I feel your hugs
Feels good

DL Saucy: where are u in front of me or in back

Lonely farmer: In back with my arms around you

DL Saucy: mmmm nice

Lonely farmer: Feels great

DL Saucy: yes

Lonely farmer: What if I snore

DL Saucy: I'll kick u

Lonely farmer: Are you going to elbow me

DL Saucy: lol

Lonely farmer: Oh kicking huh

DL Saucy: yup

Lonely farmer: Okay
You are something

DL Saucy: No I'm not

Lonely farmer: Yes you are

DL Saucy: Ok I am

Lonely farmer: Would you stop wiggling

DL Saucy: stop taking all the blankets

Lonely farmer: I m trying to sleep

DL Saucy: yeah sure u r
Get your hard off my ***

Lonely farmer: I thought u wanted it there

DL Saucy: ohh right I put it there

Now sleep
Lonely farmer: Ok nite nite xoxoxo xoxoxo
Sleep tight

DL Saucy: nite john
U too
Lonely farmer: One more good night kiss
Kiss kiss kiss

DL Saucy: k kiss kiss

That night I realized this was just one day we'd spent together. One day where I felt so close to someone, so together, and so accepted. We'd met five days earlier. That's all. Five days! And already he was all I could think about. I mean, we were sleeping together already. Sort of. This wasn't normal for me, for anyone my age with my life. But it was the most natural and fun thing I'd ever done.

It just showed me how I was beginning to realize some other force must be at work. I mean, you don't just get this close this fast. Some higher power, God, was working His way up There. What else could explain the happiness I felt, the comfort, with this flying-driving-hugging farmer in Washington, somewhere I'd never been and would probably never see. It couldn't just be coincidence, could it?

8

Donna/JP

Lonely farmer: Now you even know about my sex life or
lack thereof.
There is a lot more to life than sex.

DL Saucy: I know John but I was in a sexless marriage. I
used to cry myself to sleep many many nights And now that
I'm older I don t know what I am or what I want out of life.

I'd told Donna so much about my family, my health and, yes, my
body, that I couldn't help but wonder, what's next?

DL Saucy: somet nes I would wake up in the night and
look at him and say why can't I love this man.

Lonely farmer: Oh Donna that's terrible. What can we do
about it?
Let's work on it
How about just being happy?
Focus on your strong points

DL Saucy: but while looking for that happiness, and I want
that I do. but 3 times I loved and 3 times I lost

Lonely farmer: Donna maybe the 4th time is your time.

DL Saucy: maybe who knows
Ok enough sad stuff

Lonely farmer: Like I said don't give up
Ok no matter what

DL Saucy: I won't give up...I know

Lonely farmer: All right that's what I wanted to hear

DL Saucy: U got it, sweetheart
No giving up for me

Lonely farmer: Donna I think you are special. I think I
know you pretty good by now
You sure brighten my day

DL Saucy: Ok then get the sunshine out
oh wait that's in the morning

Lonely farmer: I'm always looking at my phone to see if
you are there

DL Saucy: Get the moonshine out
oh wait that's a, drink....lol
oh hell get it all out

Lonely farmer: I want to give you a big hug

DL Saucy: I'll take it too and give u a bigger one back

The past few days had turned my life upside down and inside out. I was feeling old and overweight and wearing Depends, but somehow God brought me this man. This person who made me feel good no matter what I told him, no matter how many of my secrets I let slip. I was sixty-seven-years-old and had only now, for the first time in my entire life, met someone who saw Me. The Real Me. The Me that I knew was in there, but who life's problems and hardships had squashed down so I wasn't sure any of her was left.

But with JP I felt safe. I felt like I could be who I was, completely vulnerable, and it would be okay. He wouldn't hurt me with it, or reject me, or say something mean. I was telling him everything about me, I mean ALL of it. And he just kept telling me how wonderful I was. No matter what. I. Told. Him. How was that even possible? That someone could . . . love . . . me and at the same time know all about me? I hadn't felt this intimate with someone for so long. Maybe never. Well, absolutely never. Not the way JP made me feel.

We began to feel so comfortable with each other, and so attracted to each other, and I don't just mean 'cause we both liked mac and cheese, that our texts took on a new path.

> Lonely farmer: I want to give you a big hug
>
> DL Saucy: I'll take it too, and give u a bigger one back
>
> Lonely farmer: Okay
>
> DL Saucy: I'm going to wait till u go to bed
>
> Lonely farmer: Ok me too
>
> DL Saucy: Then you going to tuck me in?
>
> Lonely farmer: I want to do more than tuck you in

DL Saucy: I'm gonna wash my face, brush my teeth, then I'll get comfy and u can do anything u like with me

Lonely farmer: I can do anything?

DL Saucy: Yes
Can I tell u something

Lonely farmer: Anything

DL Saucy: Now don't think badly of me

Lonely farmer: Ok I won't

DL Saucy: But when u said I want to do more than tuck you in
I started getting warm all over

Lonely farmer: So maybe I had some sort effect on you 2500 miles away. Fantastic
I'm in bed now waiting for you!!!

DL Saucy: Now move over

Lonely farmer: I'm on my side. If I move over I'll be on the floor

DL Saucy: lol ......no silly, this way move over this way

Lonely farmer: Oh okay. How is that?

DL Saucy: And tell me what makes u happy

Lonely farmer: I'm putting my arm around you

DL Saucy: Really? perfect

Lonely farmer: Talking to you makes me happy

DL Saucy: Mmmm me too

Lonely farmer: You make me feel like a teenager
I know it sounds crazy

DL Saucy: I know, and we can be teenagers, we can be
anything we want

Lonely farmer: Ok I'll be Richard Gere

DL Saucy: I can't wait to hold you
And I'll be Julia Roberts

Lonely farmer: Well you are a pretty woman

DL Saucy: Thank u
I'll be your beck and call girl

Lonely farmer: love that movie

DL Saucy: I wish I could hold you....John I want to
massage you

Lonely farmer: Me too you.....Donna you're amazing

DL Saucy: It's the wine you gave me, makes me mellow

Lonely farmer: I am laying down

DL Saucy: Ok I' I massage your back

Lonely farmer: All right. A little higher please

DL Saucy: Do u have a t shirt on?

Lonely farmer: Yes

DL Saucy: Well I'll take it off

Lonely farmer: Ok.....Now it's off

DL Saucy: John do you miss intimacy?
I don't want u to think badly of me

Lonely farmer: It's all right to be honest, and I don't think
bad of you.

DL Saucy: Ok thank you.... do you think we can be active in
the bedroom?

Lonely farmer: What could be better for 2 old over the hill
lovers
Donna you are amazing

DL Saucy: So I'm still massaging your back
Can u feel it?

Lonely farmer: Feels great. Oh yeah

DL Saucy: Your head, down your neck your shoulders
Your shoulder blades

Lonely farmer: U want me to massage you

DL Saucy: I'll run my knuckles down the middle of your back

Lonely farmer: Oh wow that feels great

DL Saucy: I'll lean over and kiss your shoulders

Lonely farmer: It feels so good

DL Saucy: First one side then the other

Lonely farmer: You're killing me

DL Saucy :   I hope so John
Turn over on your back

Lonely farmer: Ok now what

DL Saucy: I'm sitting naked next to you

Lonely farmer: Okay wow

DL Saucy: I'll lean over and press my breast against your chest

Lonely farmer: And???

DL Saucy: Kiss you on your lips

Then I'll take your hand
Place it on my breast

Lonely farmer: I ll kiss you back more

DL Saucy: Mmmmm.......nice

Lonely farmer: Feels good........your putting thoughts and visions in my head. And I love it

DL Saucy: Mmm now slide your hand over your tummy

Lonely farmer: Okay

DL Saucy: It's my hand

Lonely farmer: Oh yeah

DL Saucy: Mmmmm..... R u ok with this?

Lonely farmer: Yeah its fun

DL Saucy: Vision me really doing this
Now I will lie down beside you

Lonely farmer: Wow
Okay
I'll never go to sleep. Because you have me excited

DL Saucy: You won't have to sleep just yet John.....
Not right now

Lonely farmer: Wow
Okay you are turning me on

Maybe there is some life left in me

DL Saucy: What would u like right now honey ...
mmmm....anticipating your next move........mmmmm

9

Donna/JP

She was the last thing I thought of before I went to sleep and the first thing I thought of when I woke up, and I hadn't known her a week yet.

My life had gone from a hollow shell of loss, to one brimming with excitement and happiness. We'd never met, we only had vague notions of where the other lived, and we hadn't even spoken to each other. It was only texts, lots of them, revealing the details and nuances of our very souls, and the playfulness we both had lost somewhere in the many decades of our lives.

> Lonely farmer: Good morning. I'm sorry if my snoring kept you awake last night.
>
> DL Saucy: geez the least u can do is let me sleep after keeping me awake all night
>
> Lonely farmer: Can you speak up I don't have my hearing aids in
>
> DL Saucy: lol

Lonely farmer: So how did you sleep?

DL Saucy: Good, u?

Lonely farmer: Okay just woke up a few minutes ago

DL Saucy: Me too

Lonely farmer: What a nice thing waking up next to you

I wanted to get Skype or some other way of seeing each other online. I knew what Donna looked like, she was beautiful even though she didn't know it, and I wanted us to be able to see each other sometimes when we talked. Donna wasn't too excited about this. I think she was worried about what she looked like. And we were both worried about making a mistake and losing what we had. So we were stuck: how could we get closer without spoiling everything?

I had some ideas floating around, but I decided to go slowly with them. Just test the waters to see how Donna felt. What we had was amazing--I wanted more and she did too--so it became a challenge for both of us to figure out the best next steps.

Lonely farmer: What will Skype do for us

DL Saucy: we can talk on voice

Lonely farmer: Video too?

DL Saucy: perhaps

Lonely farmer: Okay

DL Saucy: I'm not sure I want that

Lonely farmer: That's ok we don't have to

DL Saucy: I know

Lonely farmer: I don't want to ruin what we have because it's special

DL Saucy: yes

Lonely farmer: Maybe we need baby steps
Although we are sleeping together

I was becoming more and more reliant on Donna. Not for anything specific, I just loved how she filled the minutes of my day. Today she had things to do, I knew that. She was going to the casino with her parents and her ex-husband would be there too. She had to get ready and do all the normal things in life, but it was like I wanted just one more breath from her, one more word or thought. And as soon as I got that one, I wanted another. And the amazing thing? She felt that way too.

Lonely farmer: I have to get up pretty soon because my back is starting to hurt

DL Saucy: Me too, its time to get up and get going

Lonely farmer: Not quite yet
A few more minutes Ok?

DL Saucy: Ok

I found I was always thinking about him. I'm at the casino, helping to look after my dad in his wheelchair, with my mom and the ex-John, and all I can think about is JP. I decide to see if he's around . . .

DL Saucy: hey u, u there?
I'm at the casino, they have wifi here

Lonely farmer: Hi I'm home and I got Skype

DL Saucy: who are u on skype

Lonely farmer: Wait
I forgot. I think it's beech guy

DL Saucy: k but I gotta go for now

Lonely farmer: Ok call me later

DL Saucy: I will ttyl dads waiting for me

It was so exciting to know he was there, waiting for me too. Any worry I had about him being for real, for leading me on to only break my heart later, was evaporating. Well, maybe not entirely, but partly. The scary thoughts, that he would leave me, or that one of us would do something stupid and spoil all this, those thoughts I pushed away. I mean, why not feel like a teenager again? Why not have silly fun and enjoy life, even if I felt rotten and wore Depends and had an ex-husband living with me. JP was okay with all that . . . he was okay with ME.

DL Saucy: Lol now we crashed a birthday party

Lonely farmer: Oh really?
DL Saucy: Lol, an old friend wanted dad to come so we

took him there
it's his 80th birthday

Lonely farmer: Wow 80 that's something

DL Saucy: yup
and well, he's got free wifi
k I gotta go again
C u later
kiss

Lonely farmer: Ok have fun
Kiss

We were working out how to talk through Skype and whatever else we could. But technology had us both baffled sometimes. The first time we managed to skype with video it didn't come in clearly so it ended up being no big deal. And I didn't know where we'd go next. It was like playing hide-and-seek. He was there, then I'd have to do something and he wasn't, but then I'd sneak in a hi and he was there. But then one day, a week into this, I saw just what a generous man he was. I mean, they don't make people like that every day.

Lonely farmer: Okay. We can text over the cell network if you want. I promise I will never call you unless you want me to. My number is ...
When you're not home, why don't u just use your phone? Maybe you don't have unlimited minutes.

DL Saucy: I dont have it as a cell phone i dont have data on it. I use it as a tablet i can use it only on wifi

Lonely farmer: Oh okay. You know we can email also. Although I like the texting. Check your email I will send you a picture of the sun coming up through smoky sky.

Smoke from forest fires.
So you can't even make a phone call?

DL Saucy: no thats why skype
we can talk on there

Lonely farmer: Donna do you want your phone turned
on? I can help if you would accept it.

DL Saucy: ohhh my god.... no hon really

Lonely farmer: It's okay I would love to help
Did you get the picture?

DL Saucy. no...... thank u ......really really thank u...but
no..John omg thank u though

Lonely farmer: Ok but if you ever need anything please
don't hesitate to ask. I really mean it.

DL Saucy: omg thank u really

Lonely farmer: Okay. Another subject-do you like
football?

DL Saucy: but don't be too generous like that online ok?
cause there are a lot of goldiggers out there and u are to
nice to easy to take advantage of.
Lonely farmer: I know that. But I think I am a pretty good
judge of you. I would never say that to anyone else. After
all someone that tells me they wear Depends has to be
special. Lol

DL Saucy: lol

Lonely farmer: What about football?

10

Donna/JP

Lonely farmer: I'm having trouble getting enough sleep. It must be your fault

I wake up and you are on my mind

Are you okay after last night?

DL Saucy: I'm ok

u?

Lonely farmer: Me too. I hope you're not just using me for sex. Ha ha

We were getting more intimate. We weren't actually having sex, or phone sex, or whatever you call it, but we were sure getting closer. I'd never experienced anything like it. And JP was such a gentleman. Well, a naughty gentleman, just the way I like them. I was touched that he checked in with me the next morning--I mean about our getting almost intimate. I knew this was new territory for both of us, and as long as we talked about it I assumed everything would be okay. Or I prayed it would. But true to JP's nature, he just kept on going like nothing was unusual about two old folks nearly having sex on the phone after only knowing each other for a few days!

And each time we took a step closer, it felt better.

And scarier.

What if he was my next broken heart, all lined up ready to shatter my life all over again? All it would take was one little thing--a wrong word or sentiment or who knew what. And this could vanish, blip! So I did the only thing I knew to do, I kept pushing him away. If my heart was going to get broken anyway, and the odds were it would, then I'd better keep some distance. I worried that he was falling too fast, and that it would lead to mistakes along the way. Mistakes that could ruin everything we had.

Lonely farmer: I now have 2 of them

DL Saucy: what? 2 adult tricycles?

Lonely farmer: 1 on the farm and 1 in Sunriver

DL Saucy: where's sunriver

Lonely farmer: Look it up on the internet. It's a resort in central Oregon. You will see it when I take you there.
I own a condo there and an airplane hangar. They have an airport right there.

DL Saucy: thats beautiful

Lonely farmer: When will you go with me
Well not today but maybe in a couple of months?
You need to live more..... besides it's no fun for me to go alone.
You wouldn't want me to be alone would you

DL Saucy: I have so many responsibilities here right now

Lonely farmer: I know but some of those responsibilities

are to YOU!! You have to let yourself try new things.

DL Saucy: I can't leave my parents right now, and although I think we know each other pretty well we need more time

Lonely farmer: You would only be gone from home as long as you would like. Maybe 4 or 5 days.
I know. I said n a couple of months.

DL Saucy: Ok

Lonely farmer: Did I mention I have a king size bed there?

DL Saucy: lol

Lonely farmer: There's a commercial airport in Rochester you know and they have these big airplanes that will take you anywhere.
And I have a car to pick you up with
Just keep it in your mind for the future okay

DL Saucy: omg John this is all so overwhelming

Lonely farmer: Well I have all these things. Wouldn't you like to share them with me before we get old?
Let yourself go. Take a chance and have some fun. Life is short. I have firsthand experience on that subject.

DL Saucy: Ohhh yes John but I just don't know what to do

Lonely farmer: Stop worrying about it.
I would wine you and dine you

DL Saucy: omg

Lonely farmer: We could meet in Vegas if you wanted.

He was pushing me to meet him, which of course I was dying to do. But then what? What would happen if we didn't like each other in person? Worse, what would happen if we did? We lived on opposite ends of the country! Would he just fly back and forth in that little plane of his? Or would we all go broke buying tickets that I couldn't afford in the first place? Whichever way I turned it around, it just didn't fit--except for one thing, our hearts fit perfectly. Like spooning in bed on a warm Sunday morning. Or the moon and the sun. How about warm chocolate on ice cream.

I kept bugging Donna to meet me in person. It was an idea that I just couldn't shake. I was in love with her, no doubt about it. I hadn't said those words, but my heart pounded with it every time I checked my phone. She had given me a new life, one I never imagined possible, and I didn't know I could care this much anymore.

But one thing I was learning fast was, she was one stubborn woman. Funny, feisty, sexy, and stubborn as hell. I'd push her to meet me, and she'd push me right back away. Again and Again. I could feel her worry, her pain. She'd been hurt by men before, for a long time, and I just needed to show her I wasn't that person. I needed her to believe me, that I was different, and the only way I could see to do that was to meet face-to-face. Then she would know that I wasn't just words, I was real. That my actions were better than my typed out texts. But how would I get her to do it?

Lonely farmer: If we did meet someday you could bring a daughter or granddaughter if it made you more comfortable.

DL Saucy: my daughter is here and she says hi to u
Lonely farmer: Hi right back at her. Which one?
She probably thinks I'm crazy

DL Saucy: Bonnie
She thinks you're not For real
lol

Lonely farmer: Ok hi Bonnie!!!
What do you think? That's all that matters

DL Saucy: Bonnie says she wants to meet u first lol. oh
boy you will like her better

Lonely farmer: Is she single???

DL Saucy: yup
see u want her right !!!lol

Lonely farmer: Wow she's a knockout!!

DL Saucy: I know

Lonely farmer: So Bonnie thinks I'm not for real?
In what way?

DL Saucy: You're too nice

Lonely farmer: Why?

DL Saucy: we got this saying .....if something seems too
good to be true...then it usually is

Lonely farmer: How can I prove it to you? I think that's

Bonnie talking not you.
You have to believe in me. I told you no BS.

If Bonnie didn't believe in me, then that's what she'd be telling Donna. It made sense though. Bonnie was her daughter, of course she'd try to protect her mom. It was the most natural thing in the world. Only problem was, Donna didn't need protecting from me, but neither of them truly knew that. We lived in a time when trust didn't come easy. Just turn on the news and you heard about murders and rapes and scams, so why wouldn't Donna and Bonnie be wary? And how did a man then prove he was honest, and a gentleman, and the kind who wouldn't rip anybody off even if he could?

DL Saucy: And now I'm thinking I am brainwashed because there are a lot of nice people in the world

Lonely farmer: Oh oh. She is probably right most of the time. You know how these internet things turn out Have some faith.

DL Saucy: I try I really try

Lonely farmer: You never know I might be one of them

DL Saucy: might be?

Lonely farmer: Sorry I am

DL Saucy: lol

Who was I to be suspicious of JP? He'd never done one thing to imply he was anything other than what he was, a sad, lonely, gentleman farmer with a great sense of humor. But just as soon as I started to believe in him, that voice in my head would warn me not to. "Remember what happened last time!" it would say. "You'll get hurt! You'll get hurt! You'll get hurt!"

I just wanted to shut the bitch up, but Bonnie was worried too, and she was a sensible girl.

I went back and forth like this, my brain swirling with happiness and worry. Until he texted me, and then everything felt right. I was butter in his hands, and it scared the hell out of me.

DL Saucy: BOO!!! IM BACK

Lonely farmer: YOU SCARED ME!!!!!!! Hi
Are you home?

DL Saucy: yes

Lonely farmer: How R your parents

DL Saucy: same

Lonely farmer: What do they think about you and me?

DL Saucy: they don't know YET
the less they know the better

And that was another issue, my parents. They were both weak and frail, and my father wasn't doing well at all. What was I doing getting involved with a man who lived two thousand miles away? I had responsibilities here that I couldn't just sweep away. My parents, my daughters, my granddaughters, and my health meant I wasn't fit for traveling anyway. It just didn't make sense . . . until he would text me again.

Then everything made sense.

> Lonely farmer: You seem to have so many feelings, very honest and intelligent. Life has not been fair to you. You deserve better.
>
> DL Saucy: It's killing me
>
> Lonely farmer: I know you keep saying that.
> Maybe our relationship will grow and give you a life. There's still time. Time will tell
>
> DL Saucy: yes maybe
>
> Lonely farmer: So I'm trying to get all this straight
>
> DL Saucy: I know that everything that happens in my life happens for a reason
> I just can't figure out why
>
> Lonely farmer: First one was a real idiot and wanted you to abort your baby right
>
> DL Saucy: ....yup
>
> Lonely farmer: Second one was kind of a marriage of convenience
>
> Third was the one you just told me about
> DL Saucy: right
>
> Lonely farmer: I wish I was there right now to give you a

big hug and k ss
You need it

DL Saucy: I th nk the first one ruined me for life
I was never the same after that

Lonely farmer: No no no
You still have time

DL Saucy: I just don't care about me anymore

Lonely farmer: You make me feel like I lead a charmed life.

DL Saucy: you do honey, you are blessed you had a
wonderful marriage you have, lovely children and
grandchildren

Lonely farmer: Then why do I hurt so bad? I've been
crying all morning

DL Saucy: Me too
I'm sorry for you truly
i am

Lonely farmer: I'm crying right now

DL Saucy: ocooooohhhhh don't

Donna and I shared more and more of our pain. We were both in
bad spots: my wife was barely gone, and Donna had health and

family issues, plus a train wreck of a love life. It was as if the only place we both had that felt good was with each other. I couldn't imagine what state I would be in if I hadn't met her. When I wasn't thinking of her, or texting or skyping with her, I was in so much pain I couldn't think straight. But when I heard my phone ding, or when she replied to me, the world just fell back into place.

Donna confessed to me her self-esteem problems. How she didn't believe she was worth anything to anyone, even herself. And I tried to talk her out of it, to show her the beautiful person she really was but just couldn't see. I wanted to help her see her real self, the beautiful, funny, sexy person I saw. But she was stubborn here too.

> Lonely farmer: I want to tell you what my therapist said so let me type
>
> DL Saucy: .....ok
>
> Lonely farmer: She said the old me is gone forever. Don't try to get him back you can't. I have to learn new things and meet new people. And it just takes time
>
> DL Saucy: .....that's true
>
> Lonely farmer: I hope meeting you is a new beginning for me and maybe for you. You need it too
>
> DL Saucy: I know I know. Wanna skype John?
> Lonely farmer: This has been a bad day for me Donna. Ashley has been gone most of the day
> I feel like I have known you a lot longer than I have Donna
> I don't know. I don't want you to see me cry. A little later. Ok?

DL Saucy: ok... t's all good john
we are friends for a reason im sure of that
I don't know where this will lead

Lonely farmer: I hope so because you have really helped
me. More than I can tell you.
I hope it leads to something real good for both of us

DL Saucy: who knows John maybe I am just your stepping
stone for someone better to come into your life

Lonely farmer: hope you're the one.

DL Saucy: maybe I am just the person to get you out of
your shell and maybe you're here to help me over my
hurdles right now
I want you to know I like you a lot..

Lonely farmer: I know you have commitments there, but
they can be worked out

DL Saucy: And I don't ever want to hurt you or break your
heart

Lonely farmer: Donna I like you a lot too

DL Saucy: so im going to be real careful for a while ok?
And you too

For a person who didn't value herself enough, Donna sure was smart. She knew we needed to be careful, and gradually I realized she was protecting us both. We were so very fragile in our own ways. Like a puff of wind could shatter either one of us, but if we were together we protected each other. We sheltered each other from the wind.

And I insisted on trying to get Donna to not beat herself up so damn much. It seemed like if I could just get her to see another side of life then her troubles could shift. She was stuck, and maybe I could help get her moving again.

DL Saucy: I know I'm an ok person
But I am always feeling like I don't belong

Lonely farmer: Stop being down on yourself
You're just stuck in a bad situation and you don't know how to get out

DL Saucy: EXACTLY

Lonely farmer: Maybe we can figure it out together

DL Saucy: But this is my whole life
my parents my kids my brothers. I don't know any other life

Lonely farmer: You can't leave your parents and it seems like they don't understand what's going on with you.

DL Saucy: no they don't
damn even my husband
they know I don't love him
It will never change

Lonely farmer: It's your life too

DL Saucy: He will continue to do what he does
John In the past I have depended on him a lot

Lonely farmer: I think he is using you with no
consideration for you or your feelings
You have needs too

DL Saucy: I cant walk far, I'm incontinent. I would be no
good to anyone

Lonely farmer: Donna you could be a great companion
Stop beating yourself up

DL Saucy: ok
I'm done
No more pity party for me
you make me smile

When Donna joked or laughed the world just lit up for me. She could get so blue, but if I worked with her, she'd turn it all around into a smile, for both of us. Not only was I realizing how careful we needed to be, it was also dawning on me how much we were beginning to rely on each other. If I was down the first thing I did was text her. I didn't want her to feel down too, I just wanted her cheerfulness to warm the frost that had settled on my heart. And I always knew when she was having a bad day or even a bad moment. I tried to be there for her just like she was for me.

11

Donna/JP

DL Saucy: you there

Lonely farmer: I'm here now

DL Saucy: I can't sleep. I'm so tired I can't sleep

Lonely farmer: Ok then talk to me
I'm tired too but I'd rather talk to you then sleep.

DL Saucy: Ok were u sleeping?

Lonely farmer: Yes but I just woke up
I missed tucking you in

DL Saucy: I had 2 margaritas today

Lonely farmer: I'm hugging you now, Can you feel my
arms around you?

DL Saucy: awww yess
I feel u huggin

Lonely farmer: When I close my eyes I can see you.

DL Saucy: really

Lonely farmer: I think we have to stop meeting in the
middle of the night
Your parents will find out

DL Saucy: uh oh

I knew what I wanted to give Donna for a gift, but I also knew she'd
say no. We'd only met a week ago, but it was like I knew her heart,
and she wasn't the type to take gifts or money or anything she felt
would take advantage of me. A lot of women wouldn't be like that.
Men too, I suppose.

But we spent so much time together now--probably more
than most married people--and I knew she needed what I had in
mind. She was on a tight budget and I had money. Not millions
and millions, but enough to take care of her a little bit, if she'd just
let me.

Which she wouldn't.

But I'd try anyway.

I guess that was part of why I was falling in love with her.
Which I knew I was. It's not every day you meet someone who's
fun and beautiful and makes you feel so good inside, AND has a
great sense of morals. Besides, it was just a small gift, and would
help us get to know each other even better. I just had to pick the
right time to tell her.

Lonely farmer: Good morning, just woke up. R U awake?

DL Saucy: Yes. U put me to sleep last night

Lonely farmer: U know only 2 margaritas to get you into
bed. Lol
I have to get up. My back is starting to hurt. I'll have my
phone close by so you can still talk to me. I might not

answer you right away.

DL Saucy: Ok m gonna get cleaned up too

Lonely farmer: Okay. Out of shower and I'm dressed and now making coffee. Would you like some coffee?

DL Saucy: yes, please

Lonely farmer: I'm in my office now. Paying some bills.

DL Saucy: yuk I hate that job
I'm going shopping today and over to my uncles tonight

Lonely farmer: Okay I wanted to see your beautiful hair and face on Skype, I understand.

DL Saucy: oh get those glasses fixed

Lonely farmer: My glasses are fine

DL Saucy: yeah yeah, sure

Lonely farmer: I'm not kidding, I mean It

DL Saucy: well thank u

Lonely farmer: Hey Donna we R both old, well me anyway, so why not a compliment now and then!

It didn't seem right to just tell her by texting. I knew she would say no, so I wanted her to understand I wasn't after anything. I was just an old guy who wanted to do something nice for her. It wasn't like it was diamonds or a marriage proposal.

But the Internet was the only way I had of contacting her.

Lonely farmer: please give me your mailing address

DL Saucy: oh i don't give out too much info over the internet

I saw what she needed, and I wanted to give it to her. So I figured with someone like Donna, I needed to let her know what I thought of her first. What I really thought and what I really felt. This way she would know it was alright. And then she could tell me no. But I had to try.

So I did what we used to do in the old days: I wrote her a letter. Except I was in too much of a hurry to actually mail it--and I didn't have her address anyway--and it was too long to text. So I emailed it to her.

Lonely farmer: Hi it's 5 my time. I'm back home.

DL Saucy: hi there sexy I'm home its 8 pm

Lonely farmer: I'm sexy? Now who needs glasses
Donna I wrote a note that is too long to text so I am going to email it to you. Please read it and text me back

DL Saucy: ok

Lonely farmer: I just sent it a few minutes ago

DL Saucy: ......well hurry up run run run

Donna,

The grief I have over the loss of my wife is almost unbearable at times. Talking and joking with you has helped me more then I can express in words to you. You have made some of my lonely days and nights bearable. For that I thank you. I don't know where our relationship will go from here but I know what you have done for me in this short period of time and it has really helped me. I hope our relationship can continue to improve and grow because I really really l ike you.

Sometimes I can't believe we met online, it seems crazy, but it works. You seem very special. Too bad we're 2500 miles apart.

Anyway just accept the DAMN gift from me and get on with it. It's only money. It's not like it's a commitment or anything.

After all we need to communicate when you're not home ha ha!! Or at least it would be nice to be able to. All I need is your address!!! So if you text me your address I will take that as a green light to proceed.

John

JP wanted to buy me a gift, but there was no way I could take it.

Lonely farmer: I'd like to send you a gift

DL Saucy: for what?
Lonely farmer: helping me thru all this sadness

DL Saucy: No way

I didn't want a payment or a gift or anything from him. I just wanted things to be the way they were. I didn't want our relationship getting strange with him buying me things and maybe expecting something in return. He had more money than I did, but I wanted us to stay the way we were.

I quickly learned how stubborn he was. He swore it didn't mean anything and wouldn't change what we had. And he simply Would. Not. Let. Up. At. All.

He told me he spent an entire hour composing the letter that he emailed me, and his feelings would be hurt if I didn't take the gift. Actually, the *damn* gift. I figured his feelings would be okay, but the letter was beautiful. It came from the heart, I could tell. So I said yes, finally. And I must have cried too because it was such a nice thing to do for someone.

DL Saucy: Do you know my name?

Lonely farmer: Donna Licata is that right?
Do I have the name right Donna?

DL Saucy: yes

Lonely farmer: Okay now that wasn't so hard was it?

DL Saucy: I really feel funny about this

Lonely farmer: Donna I'm an old guy that has some

money. So why not use it to make someone's day

DL Saucy: Please I dont want gifts John. I am just happy
to smile again cause I know what its like to be in that dark
hole.

Lonely farmer: I know but I like to do it. It makes me feel
good
Enough of the mushy stuff. Let's talk about something
else.

I was thinking he was going to send me flowers or candy or a gift
certificate or something like that. So when I got a box through the
mail I sat for a bit and stared at it. My daughter kept saying "Open it,
open it!" and I have to admit I liked getting the gift. But at the same
time I was confused about what to do.

Finally, I opened the box and was shocked to find an iPhone
inside. He'd mentioned wanting to be able to talk to me anytime,
but the expense ...I was quite sure the gift had cost at least one
hundred dollars. But when I mentioned it to my granddaughter
Gabby she laughed.

"No way, Grandma. That's a thousand-dollar phone."

"He must have spent his whole social security check on me. I
can't keep it."

"Why?"

"Would you?"

"It's a gift."

"But it's so *expensive*."

She rolled her eyes and I got on the computer to tell JP I
couldn't keep his lovely gift and would send it back to him.

He would not let me do that. We had our first spat, I suppose.
It wasn't much, but it went on a bit and JP expressed some
frustration.

Lonely farmer: you wouldn't give me your phone number
so I gave you one

DL Saucy: LOL

He was clever. His gift would move our relationship forward, in an amazing way, and provide the kind of intimacy that helped create more trust in the powerful connection we had made.

But gifts were hard for me to accept because knowing JP was its own reward. I didn't want to be bought or wooed by an expensive stuff.

So throughout the afternoon I remained stubborn. Finally, JP said that if I returned the phone he would send it again. That meant I would have to buy postage a second time to ship the phone back. That kind of thing would cut a big whole in my budget.

By 6 o'clock that evening my daughter Bonnie had weighed in.

"Keep it, Mom."

"But what kind of example would that be after always telling you kids never take a gift from strangers?"

"But you like this man, don't you?"

"Yes."

"And he hasn't asked you to send him money for some crazy reason, has he?"

"He'd never do that."

"How do you know?"

I just knew and told her so. "He's not that kind of man."

"Then keep the phone. Otherwise you might hurt his feelings and never hear from him again."

She nailed it. That was my biggest fear--losing him--not getting ensnared in some sort of "pay-to-play" scam. LOL.

There was a kind of silence between JP and me that day. An uncomfortable silence. But then he called me on the iPhone with FaceTime and I loved being able to see him and talk face-to-face. He practically begged me to keep the phone.

"I can't afford the minutes, JP," I said. It was an excuse to send back the gift.

But he had a comeback.

"Donna, I already paid for all that. Do you think I'd send you a phone and they ask you to pay for the minutes?"

I wondered how I would ever be able to thank him for it, but he told me it was just a gift and not to worry about it. I had been so worried it would change things between us, but I hadn't needed to. JP was so sweet, and we got back to our normal chatting right away. I think he knew I was sensitive about it, so he made sure nothing changed in the tone and manner of our communications.

And truthfully, I quickly grew fond of my new cell. It was smooth and shiny and I was excited to learn how to get the most out of it.

Before meeting my Prince Charming I began to write a book. It was an attempt to turn my all-too-real life experiences into fantasy. Yet here I was sitting in my kitchen on a phone I never could have afforded talking with a lovely man who wanted me to be happy. My fantasy novel was now turning into real life.

As I sat there glowing and laughing with JP, I recalled our conversation about my wish to write.

> Lonely farmer: what type of book will it be don't give up keep trying.
>
> DL Saucy: I'm taking my life experiences and turning it into a fantasy.
>
> Lonely farmer: what a great idea.
>
> DL Saucy: I have lots of ideas and notes and outlines. I started out looking out my window up at the star Orion? you know the star Orion? The rest is a fantasy that I haven't really figured out total yet.

Lonely farmer: I do know Orion. If you keep trying it will probably work out.

DL Saucy: yes you could see that star from both sides of the world so two people at the end of the world can both be watching Orion at the same time.

Lonely farmer: exactly

DL Saucy: I hope it happens I'm really excited.

Lonely farmer: I know it won't happen unless you keep trying.

DL Saucy: right

Lonely farmer: don't give up trying.

In our first iPhone conversations we covered so much ground. Conversing, gabbing, was a lot easier than texting; and it confirmed our ease with one another. Hearing each other's voices didn't dampen the thrill, it accelerated our desire to advance our relationship.

"Donna, this connection is very important to me. I know you didn't want a gift for communicating, but at a time in my life when I really needed something or someone to talk with you were there."

"But you're still talking with your psychiatrist, aren't you?"

"Grief counselor. Oh, yeah. But that's different. When I sent the phone I knew you didn't like accepting gifts. But it never occurred to me that it would create some tension."

He confessed his feelings would have truly been hurt. Sigh of relief: I avoided that catastrophe, and was reminded that JP was still tender. He'd suffered a terrible loss. By this time in our relationship, his wife Shirley had only been gone about three weeks. Of course the rejection of his kindness would have stung.

But we recovered and began to use the text function on our phones every chance we got, just like we'd been doing online. In no time at all we were back to being two little kids.

One day he had some family over and sent me a picture of them all watching TV. They looked so comfortable and family-like. I was happy he had such good people around him. Yet even on those occasions, he and I still couldn't get enough of each other.

> DL Saucy: hey u want to text quietly, we can type and not talk
>
> Lonely farmer: Okay I will call you

As JP and I got closer, I worried sometimes about him finding out something about me and not liking it. Just normal worries for a woman, I suppose, but I still wanted to protect what we had. So I figured the best way was to tell him everything I could. That way if he stopped being interested in me it would only hurt . . . a lot. A whole damn lot. But it wouldn't be like we'd taken a next step in our relationship and then have it happen.

So that day I told him I'd moved twenty-three times, and the average person only moved three times. I think he was more worried about what I was going to tell him than the fact I'd moved so much. The thing was, after I got married I moved back home every time I left my husband, which was about ten times. And when I was with him he spent all the money we made on his dreams that never panned out. So we moved then too. I wanted JP to understand I'd made some bad choices in my life, but I wasn't blaming anyone for them. They were my own--I'd made the mistakes all by myself.

I made sure JP understood that John--the ex-husband John-- was always around because he was a friend of my parents and a big help to them. My father especially was getting weaker and weaker; we made sure someone was always with him. This all led to a lot of stress and emotional baggage that I needed to make sure JP understood. I didn't want any surprises for him, because we were heading closer and closer, and I didn't want us to end up like two trains going toward each other on the same track!

> Lonely farmer: Donna don't give up. You are not old. Let yourself live.
>
> DL Saucy: I know but it's easier to give up sometimes then it is to fight
> But Hey I am a survivor
>
> Lonely farmer: Please don't give up
>
> DL Saucy: no I won't
> actually John I can't believe I am telling u all this

Donna had finally accepted the gift, which took a lot longer than I thought it would. But I respected her for her wariness, with all she'd been through. So once I won this small battle, another plan began to hatch. But this one I knew for sure would take a long time to get her to agree to. Might as well start.

> DL Saucy: how many trips have you taken in your life?
>
> Lonely farmer: A lot of trips to Reno and Vegas. None out of the country except for Canada
> How about you?
>
> DL Saucy: only Florida, Connecticut, Atlantic city, Niagara falls

Lonely farmer: Want to go to Vegas?
It's fun

DL Saucy: what's fun? Vegas.? well it may be fun if u have money to gamble with

Lonely farmer: You don't need to gamble there. There are some great shows to see
Hey you know if our relationship continues we have to meet in person some day

DL Saucy: We will talk more later I gotta get going for now
there's a lot we Will talk about

Lonely farmer: Oh that sounds serious

DL Saucy: No that's no fun being good. now I wanna be bad

Lonely farmer: Only with me hah

DL Saucy: Bye for row

Lonely farmer: Ok kiss kiss

DL Saucy: Kiss kiss
kiss

Lonely farmer: Wow 3

DL Saucy: lcl ...ok here's one more ....KISS

Before I met Donna, I'd decided to go to a therapist to help me with my grief over losing Shirley. Although I certainly felt better having met Donna, I figured it was still a good idea to get some help. It was just a matter of talking to a professional person who knew a lot about grief and sadness and who could help make sure I got better. What I didn't realize was just how much Donna knew about therapists and all the pain they'd been helping her through.

Lonely farmer: I want to talk about my visit to my therapist

DL Saucy: ok, go on

Lonely farmer: I told her about you

DL Saucy: and?

Lonely farmer: She said she was going to suggest exactly what we are doing
So what do you think about that?

DL Saucy: I think she is one smart person.... now is this the grief counseling
Lonely farmer: Yes

DL Saucy: you know that doc I went to today

Lonely farmer: Yeah what about it

DL Saucy: she is a therapist
I see her every 2 weeks
for the last 30 years
for depression

Lonely farmer: Oh wow. Does she help you?

DL Saucy: absolutely she helps. I do all the talking
she just helps me to understand what I am feeling and
why

Lonely farmer: Kinda the same with mine
I've never had one before
I think it's helping me

DL Saucy: when I cry I don't know why I am crying

Lonely farmer: Why did you say you can't believe you're
telling me these things?

DL Saucy: I don't really talk about my illnesses or
problems

Lonely farmer: I will tell you anything about me that you
want to know. No secrets
It's okay

DL Saucy: I'm trying to do that. I am tired of living a lie
but I just don't know what the truth is anymore

Lonely farmer: Together we can help each other

DL Saucy: that sounds wonderful....I have pretended for
so long to be happy
I always put on a happy face because it does help
sometimes
but as soon as I am behind closed doors I spend hours
crying

Lonely farmer: Well all I can tell you is that you are making me happier than I was before us

DL Saucy: that makes me happy

Lonely farmer: No more crying. Okay?

DL Saucy: I feel good lately

I had no idea Donna had suffered so much over the years. You just don't know what people go through unless they're really willing to open up to you. I was grateful that she was willing to do that with me. I would have told her anything at all. I wanted to take away her pain but I didn't know how. All I did was buy her a silly phone and she was so happy. But money didn't buy happiness, I knew that for a fact. So I was just there for her, to be with her, and she made me feel so good too.

Lonely farmer: I wish we lived closer

DL Saucy: I know

Lonely farmer: But there are airplanes you know

DL Saucy: lol

Lonely farmer: Not a joke

DL Saucy: ......hmmmm wonder where I can find one

Lonely farmer: I mean a commercial like Delta

DL Saucy: John I fell in love before with someone I met online and I was heartbroken

Lonely farmer: Well I said don't give up
Donna you are a good person. I can tell from our
conversations

Lonely farmer: So don't give up

DL Saucy: thank u soo very much

Lonely farmer: Allow yourself to live and have new
experiences
It's a great world out there
Take chances
Don't be afra d

DL Saucy: I want to but I am scared

Lonely farmer: Maybe I can help

DL Saucy: maybe u can

Lonely farmer: I know you have had some rotten breaks
but don't quit

DL Saucy: I won't....I am not a quitter

Lonely farmer: ....Good
I still want you to teach me to dance

JP told me that the best part of his day was talking to me, and I felt the same. We had so much in common and even when we didn't it didn't matter. He liked the Seattle Seahawks, I loved the Buffalo Bills through and through. He liked iceberg lettuce and I didn't. Who cared?

He kept hinting now that we needed to meet in person, and I kept putting him off. First of all, where would we meet? We lived 2,500 miles apart! Second, there was no way I was letting him buy me a ticket anywhere. The phone was enough.

But most importantly, what if it didn't work out? What if I didn't like him? Or him me? Then we'd lose everything we'd spent these days building up. I was already falling for him big time, and I knew he was too. Which is what was so scary. Every man I'd ever fallen for had broken my heart. Was JP different? Who knew?

Lonely farmer: I know I need several more months of recovery time. So will you wait????

DL Saucy: I need to lose a lot of weight and that will take time

Lonely farmer: I don't want some other guy sweeping you off your feet
Ok you got 2 months

DL Saucy: that's good john cause we will get to know each other better

Lonely farmer: .....okay you got 2 months

DL Saucy: and who knows John u may meet someone else also
u need to experience things too
Lonely farmer: ....Oh I don't know

DL Saucy: no decisions for a year they say..no moving no selling no buying no nothin for about a year

Lonely farmer: C< no decisions for a year. Will you wait? We have to meet way before a year

DL Saucy: we'll see

Lonely farmer: I con't want to wait a year to meet. You know nothing serious

I'd told JP about all my loves, and so I asked him about his. Of course he told me everything. because he was like that. He met his wife when he was in California working in a gas station as a mechanic. She was a customer, they dated for less than a year and got married for happily ever after. Completely the opposite to my experiences. How does it work out so well for some people and just terrible for others?

When he met his wife she had six children already and was 26 years old, six years older than he was. But it didn't matter. He'd gotten a girl pregnant in high school, but didn't have much of a relationship with that child. So he and his wife had a child together and he adopted her six kids. The more I got to know him, the more I realized he was such a good man. Six kids? And they must have all been little. Screaming and diapers and all of it, but he took them in.

DL Saucy: did u have a good happy marriage?

Lonely farmer: : has been very good. We never fought and never cheated. It couldn't have been better.
DL Saucy: you know all my loves I think

Lonely farmer: No talking about it..... I start crying

DL Saucy: .....that is awesome very very rare

Compare that to my loveless marriage. Life just hands us out different dishes. JP got a good one, and I got a terrible one. But at least for now we had each other. And we spent more and more time together, texting and learning about each other. I think he was concerned about my health because he told me how he'd lost forty pounds once, just by watching what he ate. If only it was that easy. I told him what happened when I lost weight too . . .

DL Saucy: I was 320 lbs. I am now down to 260 ...by doing just that too, eating good food and less.....I got a good one for you though.... I was always heavy so at about 35 I started losing weight, got really healthy, was energetic, happy, working out every morning ..going to work ..dancing every night.
WHAM.... phone call from the doc
you got stage 2 carcinoma melanoma something....some kind of cancer
.....ohhh but I was sooo healthy
sooooo needless to say I put it back on again

Lonely farmer: Wow

DL Saucy: But years later I wasn't happy again sooo
I lost weight
and get ready cause now you have another stage something or other kind of uterine cancer

Lonely farmer: Wow

DL Saucy: so I put the weight on again

Lonely farmer: Well don't give up it can be done

DL Saucy: .....and here I am again losing the weight
but I told the doc that I won't accept any calls bout cancer
so don't call me. IF I get it again I will live with whatever I
get now

Lonely farmer: I hope you don't have any more

DL Saucy: and that's all there is so let's talk about happy
things

Lonely farmer: We could work out together!!

No matter what I told JP, he was fine with it. He was kind and gentle with me in everything I'd done or experienced. I told him I was overweight, he was fine. He even wanted to help me lose weight and work out together. If I told him I'd had cancer he was supportive there too.

And then, he would tell me about his life and the amazing things he'd done. He and his wife and been into drag racing. Drag Racing! He had some kind of supergas car that he drove all over the country, from the west coast to Texas to Florida. He competed and got third place in the entire world. My JP.

Lonely farmer: What are you wearing?

DL Saucy: a black sundress

Lonely farmer: Sounds sexy

DL Saucy: sounds better than flannel pajamas huh?

Lonely farmer: Yes

DL Saucy: ok....you don't have to answer this
but when's the last time u had intimacy

Lonely farmer: About 3 or 4 years ago. Donna you can ask
me anything Its OK

DL Saucy: I just wondered how it's been for you

Lonely farmer: It's okay I miss it but what can you do?
I can't take Viagra or anything like that because of my
heart.

DL Saucy: I understand, how is your heart

Lonely farmer: My heart is in A fib like I told you before so
I have to take warfarin to prevent blood clots. Other than
that it's ok. No bypass or stents

DL Saucy: cool

12

Donna

Conversing on my new iPhone was a thrill, but using FaceTime blew my mind. It reminded me of the virtual reality depicted in "The Jetsons," an animated television sitcom that was popular in 1962. How we laughed when the characters would talk to each other via TV screens. More than 50 years before, some creative people were imagining what I'd be experiencing in 2015.

Not that the technological advance didn't arrive with some expectations: I was self-conscious about my looks, and I could no longer hang out in my pajamas. Now I had to dress well and comb my hair before answering the phone.

Yet our first FaceTime conversation was so normal and natural that I felt like we were together in the same room. We could share sweet, common things: JP began watching me put on my makeup in the morning. Keeping the phone had been the right decision; it had become an essential part of my life, an absolute necessity. No more lonely nights.

That first night we talked for about thirty minutes then hung up because we had chores to do and dinner to prepare. We both hurried through those obligations so that we could resume our chat.

Mostly, we talked about the phone because neither of us had much experience with FaceTime. We had a lot to learn and it was wonderful making discoveries together.

But it started getting late for me, that first night. In the East it was about 11 p.m., whereas it was only 8 p.m. in the West. And we had been talking for about four hours. So we opted to hang up for twenty minutes, get ready for bed, and then re-dial so that we could say a proper goodnight.

A routine developed. We'd talk all afternoon, stop to do errands and tasks, then talk a little more, and then stop so that we could get ready for bed, and then kiss-kiss, 'nighty-night.'

Also, our evenings were often wrapped around listening to the fabulous 1950's music that we both loved. It was a melodic way to tuck each other in and drift off into sweet dreams.

Technology sounds so cold and complicated for some people. For us the word took on new meaning and depth. The modern conveniences allowed us to court each other. Each FaceTime chat was a date, a hot-wire jolt, a love-me-tender memory.

JP would often remark that if not for the smart phones our texting through the online platform might not have allowed us to advance our level of communication and get to know each other so intimately.

"Just watching each other do things is so great," he said. "Simple things, day-to-day chores, as we talk it's like we're actually running our errands together."

Also, we no longer needed the short-hand abbreviations used online--LOL, BTW, BRB--because we could experience mannerisms and facial expressions. A smile, a smirk, a wink, these were telling signs of our enjoyment of one another. They were a code, a secret way of communicating, and it developed because we could now eat a meal together and watch how each other dressed.

Once in the grocery store, JP asked "What are we having for dinner tonight?" No matter where I shopped, my guy could be there and take part in the expedition.

I even shared the letters and packages I'd receive through the mail. Sometimes more gifts from JP.

But the big moment came when JP said, "I'd like to meet your family and friends." No problem. FaceTime gatherings became a fun part of our days and nights together.

How smart Bonnie and Gabby had been about the phone.
Keep it, Mom.

JP and I talked about this too, the phenomenon of technology, and how it had saved us both from utter despair and loneliness. Our relationship had grown by leaps and bounds within a matter of days and weeks, even though we had never actually touched; that would have to wait another couple months. Yet we were enjoying and exploring all the stages of a true romance.

"Donna, where would we be without all this?" JP said one night.

The thought made me shudder.

Our connection was not just about love. It had brought us both back to life and society. And for me, it was a chance to learn how to dream. Before meeting JP, I wasn't sure I knew how.

Possibilities. I now sensed a lot of possibilities. I was so happy that my happiness made me feel guilty.

Why did I deserve this?

13
JP

Lonely farmer: I want to be friends with someone who is close to my age

In the mid-1960s, Shirley and I were living in the San Fernando Valley, in Los Angeles County. She was a bit older than me and was already the mother of six children when we married; in the years to come I would father a child of our own. I paid the bills working for my parents in Burbank. They operated a food supplement business that sold vitamins and other products to health food stores and chiropractors. But my new wife and I decided that the Antelope Valley near Palmdale, further north, would be a better place to raise kids.

When we moved we had horses and other animals that fed on alfalfa hay. I bought the hay from a farmer near Lancaster. He became a friend and soon I developed an interest in running a farm of my own. I was mechanically inclined, enjoyed the machines, and liked the freedom of being far beyond the city limits. I began working with my friend on weekends, without pay, just to learn.

My apprenticeship lasted about a year until I met a Los Angeles man who had a farm of about 640 acres nearby. He needed someone to manage his stretch of land, so I signed on. The position allowed me to take the reins, so to speak, while still staying close to my friend and mentor who was a deep well of knowledge.

One thing lead to another. As I progressed it was clear that I had an aptitude for the work and wanted my own place. Unfortunately, farmland in California was really expensive, so it was a tough place to break in. Also, water was always tight. Although my employer owned 640 acres, his water supply was adequate for only about 164.

I explored other possibilities and discovered that the farm community in Washington state was wide open, and land was relatively cheap.

Even better, the region enjoyed an unlimited supply of water from the Columbia River that was generously refilled annually by the snow melt in Canada. It was the only area in the West that was never short of irrigation water.

It didn't take long to locate a property near Pasco, Washington. We bought the farm in 1970 with the financial help of my parents. Shirley and I worked the land side-by-side for twelve years, then sold it and bought a larger farm further north in Mesa. Our new home fronted a road named Greenacres.

One thing leads to another. That's how life had always worked for me. And that's how it seemed to be happening with Donna.

We met online and immediately felt at home with each other. Her texts were nurturance, as generous as the water ways that kept my farm abundant. When we quickly outgrew the online platform that linked us together I purchased a smart phone so that we could progress.

Now we were on a whole new level, and within a couple weeks of sharing lots over FaceTime, I wanted more.

My first inclination was to invite her to the farm. But then I turned my sights on Las Vegas which I had mentioned traveling to after sending Donna the iPhone.

Slow down, she said, we're moving too fast.

Bring Bonnie to escort you, if you want.

I don't know.

Give it some thought, I said.

FaceTime gave us everything you could want in a relationship except the nearness that would consummate our union.

Not that we didn't do everything possible to connect physically. Phone sex was now an option, but in the beginning it was mostly comic; we were laughing all the time. It tickled us to talk about touching and what we'd like to do someday in bed together.

The turn-on for us, though, was not necessarily "naughty" talk, which at first could feel awkward or a little weird. It was the mutual agreement that we wanted more of each other, so a mere "good night" at the end of our marathon conversations was not enough. We preferred to tuck each other in, so to speak, and that was a hoot because it frequently extended our talks another thirty minutes or so. Shakespeare was right. "Parting is such sweet sorrow."

The fact was we were comfortable and felt safe with each other from day one of our relationship. So exposing our true feelings was easy and natural. With our smart phones we talked our way into a mindful, intimate place that elevated us to a place that we finally came to describe as spiritual. As vague as that might sound, it was the only word we knew to explain the improbability of finding each other at such a critical time in our lives.

Despite the new horizons FaceTime provided, we also talked about withholding something so that our first meeting--Las Vegas or wherever--would be meaningful and unique. When our conversations got too hot and intense, we reminded each other of the grace of abstinence.

Also, actual intercourse suggested a level of commitment. Was it too soon to include such a word in our conversations? Donna and I knew that love had found us. We had been swept away after my first innocent and naïve introduction.

It was now one month later and I was in a state of bliss if I was talking with Donna.

Yet the previous month I had been in the hospital intensive care unit bending over my lovely wife of fifty-two years. I had been struggling to come to terms with what had just happened, because ten days ago she had developed a bleed in her brain. The doctors had told me there was no hope of recovery.

She had often told me that she had no wish to linger or be sustained by artificial means, and I made the decision to honor Shirley's wishes. If it was her time to go . . .

I was left to make the final call on her behalf. I'd made many important decisions in my life. One thing leads to another. This was agony. It felt as though I was casting her off, setting her adrift. The cruel finality cut me deeply. To be true to Shirley, I was forced to plunge myself into the darkest sadness I would ever know; a grief I was not sure that I could survive.

And now, a month later I was thinking, *Viva Las Vegas*. Was I mad to even entertain the notion of being with another woman so soon?

In fact, one reason Donna cautioned me about meeting was her concern for my need to mourn my loss so that guilt didn't continue to batter me. She may not have realized that I feared suffering a second loss. But then I realized that losing Donna because I was trying to adhere to some unwritten rule about a respectful period of mourning was foolish. Admittedly, she had arrived with the speed of lightning. Yet however inconvenient the timing might have seemed, without her companionship I don't know how long it would have taken to be rescued from the dungeon of my grief.

When Shirley and I had moved our family to the Antelope Valley in the 1960s, it wasn't only for the children. I enjoyed it too. Liberated from the drudgery of urban demands, I discovered a wholesome, fulfilling way of life that abundantly provided for our every need.

Farming was not my only success. I also became a pilot, bought my own aircraft, and competed in the Supergas class in the National Hot Rod Association (NHRA). I won the prestigious Division Championship in 2000. My love of machinery, speed, and achievement earned me much in life.

One thing leads to another.

Now I was learning that love was really no different than farming, flying, and drag racing. We reap and we sow. Shirley was taken from me, then Donna was given to me.

I thought, *Let the gods fault me, if they must. But I want to meet Donna--soon.*

14

Donna

My friends still relied on me to help them with their hair. My salon skills may have seemed cliché--I was a talkative Italian-American hairdresser--but the social aspects of my work were fun and nourishing. Since my health was not so good, a few gals would gather at my place so that we could gab and gossip while I trimmed, colored, and coiffed.

On one occasion I did a lot of listening and laughing. But when it was my turn to spill my thoughts I hesitated. Telling everyone that I'd met the love of my life online might have sounded foolish. Might? It *did* sound foolish, crazy, whatever. Yet I didn't want anyone to say that I should give up my guy.

My guy. As much as I liked the sound of that, I was at a crossroads. JP was pursuing a rendezvous in Las Vegas, which sounded divine and frightening. My guy enjoyed rolling the dice a bit. He'd spent time in casinos, obviously had some pocket change to spare, and would be familiar with the surroundings.

So what next? Las Vegas, London, Paris? It didn't matter where we met. Most any place would give me the romantic jitters. The real dilemma for me was religious.

The more I told my friends about the relationship, the more details they wanted.

"Well, I liked him before I loved him."

That's good, they all agreed.

"And I don't expect anything from him."

What? Why not? Get something in return for your--

"I mean, I don't want him to think I'm a gold digger."

They looked around my house, then back at me and asked, where are you stashing all the goodies?

We laughed because they all knew me to be frugal and not the kind of woman to be manipulative in an attempt to get my hands on riches.

"Okay, this is what I'm trying to say. I'm religious. I'm Catholic. And it's all happening so fast."

Praise the Lord. You should wait until you're seventy?

"I know, I know. Miracles happen fast. But I get confused, wondering if this is a gift from God or the Devil. Ya know?"

The girls all seemed stumped, except the BFF who was sitting in my pretend salon chair. She turned around to face me with such a serious look that I feared I'd put too many curls in her 'do.

"The Devil doesn't know love, Donna."

Jackpot. That's how my friend's words hit me. Just like the little bit of fun I'd had with the slot machines in the Canadian casinos beyond Niagara Falls. Every now and then I'd pull the arm, watch the symbols spin, and then suddenly hear coins pouring into my cup. The only difference was how you reacted. In a gambling hall you shouted. In my kitchen doing everybody's hair I was profoundly moved, dumbstruck, by the truth and simplicity of her insight. Of course. *The Devil doesn't know love.*

We all pray for amazing things to happen and then when they do we doubt or fear embracing our good fortune. In the weeks and months that followed, as I accepted God's grace, or luck, or whatever we might call it--yeah, a miracle--I would witness so much change in myself and others as life swirled with new luster.

Someone very close to me had always identified with the lesbian community. Yet one day she met a guy, they began to date, and now they planned to marry. I loved her either way, of course, but her happiness at experiencing something new and unexpected was wonderful to behold.

My daughter was tired of spending so much time alone (Or with me. Can you blame her? LOL) and longed for a relationship as JP and I grew close. She's now engaged and who knows where that will lead.

Had my life changes helped bring about other events? Is that all we needed--a little nudge or envy or surprise to make us think in new ways? To accept new possibilities?

I had lost my faith and then it was renewed. It made me wonder why I had given up. Spiritual stuff was happening all the time; it was all around us. Why didn't we notice?

Still torn about my speedy relationship with JP, I reviewed the past decade or so and realized I'd fallen into habits. The things I did each day did not come from conviction; I did them "just because" that's what I had always done. Life was just going through the motions. Even before meeting JP I became aware of the need to change. The desire to change. I wanted to try to get to know God again.

One day while visiting my parents, I was sitting on the couch in the living room with my ex-husband John. I looked out a small diamond-shaped window at the top of the front door and saw what looked like the face of Christ. I said, "John, look out that little window and tell me what you see."

He stared for a moment and then said, "I see the face of Christ." I got chills.

Eager for more proof, I called my very religious grandmother who lived on another floor in the same house and asked her to join me. She took one look at the window and announced, "There is God, without question."

Three very different people had come to the same conclusion. Yet an uncle who was there that day saw nothing but a dirty window.

"You're crazy," he said.

Fine. I was crazy, I thought as I sat in my home fondling my new iPhone. Crazy to see Christ through a dirty window, and crazy to be in love with a man who lived on the other side of the country.

Believe, Donna.

15

Donna

If I was still hesitant about meeting JP in Las Vegas it didn't stop me from introducing him to my family. In fact, FaceTime gave us a head start on blending our families. We could share gatherings and have fun together. Everybody seemed to enjoy the unique experience.

Then we encountered a new challenge. It should not have come as a surprise. JP had suffered a death in the family, and now it was my turn.

Dad passed away on August 27th, 2015, about one month after JP and I met online and just six weeks after Shirley's funeral. My new love had generously thanked me for helping him through his grief. Now it was my turn to lean on him. He did not let me down.

My use of FaceTime then was nearly obsessive. I spent every minute I could with him because I felt so lost. I loved my father, and in his late years we lived under one roof. Unlike other adult children who live far way, I interacted with Mom and Dad regularly. To say goodbye left a gaping hole in my life.

Through it all, JP was my strength. He soothed my sorrow and willingly helped with all the arrangements I needed to make. He even helped me write the eulogy that I would read at Dad's funeral and then coached me. This was a big deal, because I'm not the type of person who wants to get up in front of people. I'm not a stage performer.

Throughout the preparations and then the burial I was in the midst of another transformation. Dad had always been my Prince Charming. He'd helped me through difficult times and made me feel worthy. Now that he was gone, I was feeling less attached to Rochester, adrift you might say, with a gentle wind pushing me closer to JP. Like my dad, he seemed to instinctively know what I needed, and was more than willing to provide it.

Viva Las Vegas.

16

JP

Oh boy, now I'd done it. My mission to get Donna to accept the gift of an iPhone was successful, and it had taken us to new levels of connectedness with the sad passing of her father. Neither of us could deny the impact.

But that wasn't enough. Oh, no. Mr. High-Flying pilot needed to continue the ascent. My invitation to meet in Las Vegas had been gentlemanly, I hoped, but persistent. And true to form, in the early going, Donna had resisted.

I can't afford that! She'd said.

I insisted on paying for her airfare. No big deal. But she had other worries.

I must be crazy for thinking about flying to meet a stranger I met online, she'd said.

So I urged her to bring her daughter Bonnie as a chaperone.

Two of us? I can't afford that!

I insisted on paying for both airfares. It was only money. It's not like it's a commitment or anything, I told her.

Was I some rich guy flashing his cash, trying to impress? No. It was just that the chance to meet the woman whose company I enjoyed so much was priceless.

Regardless, when my long-distant sweetheart accepted my offer to meet in Sin City, an old adage came to mind: Be careful what you wish for.

Yes, I'll admit it. As our rendezvous grew closer, I began to have some concerns. What had I done? Would I like her in person as much as I liked her at a distance? Could I overlook her weight and other health issues? I fought these worries by reminding myself that her personality and generous emotional support were far more important measures of character.

Then I had the opposite worry: Would she like me? Maybe we wouldn't click. I thought I was in love with her, but how could that be? It all happened so fast online, and yet we had never met in person.

My anxiety widened: Would my family accept her? Did I care if they accepted her? Of course, as mentioned, I'd already wrestled with these issues after texting with Donna. But face to face, not just FaceTime at a distance, could change everything.

Despite my concerns, Donna and I continued to visit every day on our phones. At one point I asked her if she had enough clothing for the trip.

"Oh yeah. I have three outfits," she said.

Hm. That didn't sound like enough, so I decided to do something about it. A little research revealed that Donna had a Dress Barn clothing store in her area. So I went to my local outlet and bought her a $500 gift certificate and put it in the mail.

Another gift. Oh me oh my. I hoped this wouldn't cause another crisis. I also sent her my credit card number so that she could buy some items online, mostly from Amazon.

As it turned out, she had a ball and even took me along on one of her shopping sprees. Well, sort of. Donna had been reminded of the movie *Pretty Woman,* and while I was on FaceTime with her shopping, she quoted a line from it for the sales lady on my behalf: "I have an obscene amount of money to spend on her so you need to do some major sucking up." The sales lady had laughed, in part because Donna was wearing the Julia Roberts hat that I had bought her previously. My joy was in watching and hearing her delight at being able to get out of the house and spend a little fun money.

Can't buy me love? That's what the song says. Maybe it sounds like I was shelling out big bucks to woo Donna, but the truth was quite different. She had never asked for or demanded anything material from me. Gifts embarrassed her, and I found her humility enchanting. All she wanted was the truth about my life and feelings. Her message was simple and powerful: All you need is love.

That's probably why I decided to make another kind of investment several weeks before our October 28, 2015 appointment with fate. I was checking my return-home flight arrangements when I noticed only two seats were still available on my plane. A new wildfire of worry began to spread through me: Even though I knew she had tickets with Bonnie to return to New York, I needed to ensure that there were two seats available in case she accepted my invitation to come to Washington with me.

Problem solved. I purchased both seats as insurance. A gamble, sure, but despite my occasional flare-ups of doubt, I was feeling lucky.

On the morning I left my farm for the airport to fly to Las Vegas I was in good spirits. I'd gone online to check the departure times and was pleased that there were no delays. We'd all arrive in Las Vegas with plenty of time to enjoy the evening and get to know each other.

Yet my flight was not as peaceful as I had hoped it would be. Emotional turbulence came in the form of renewed apprehension about finally meeting Donna.

Then guilt slammed against me like a flock of geese. It was as if my wife Shirley was seated next to me, unaware that I intended to betray her with another woman. My mind was in a downward spiral, at times questioning the need to meet someone new.

What if it doesn't work out?

What if it does?

But I'm taking a big chance.

Nothing risked, nothing gained.

Most of the trip to Vegas was a mental boxing match. Fortunately, my feelings for Donna were so strong they eventually overrode the dark nonsense that I was having an affair. Me? A man who had never thought twice about another woman throughout his long married life?

Even Shirley came to my rescue. I imagined looking into her eyes, a fine woman now forever gone from this world. Her faint beautiful smile gently implored me to carry on with life.

Find some happiness, darling.

I jolted when the plane touched down on the tarmac. Terra firma. Welcome to Las Vegas. The gambling capital of the world.

Roll the dice, Romeo.

17

Donna

Flight plans were made to be broken. The travel day had turned into a long ordeal. But so what? After landing in Las Vegas I was so excited I considered getting out of my wheelchair and walking to meet JP.

No so fast, Honey. Trekking from one end of the airport to the other? I don't think so. My heart was pumping--I couldn't wait to see my man in person for the first time--but my body was exhausted from the delays and stopovers.

So I asked a skycap to push me toward the baggage area where we were all supposed to meet. I was wearing the big floppy hat JP had bought me that looked like the one Julia Roberts wore in the movie *Pretty Woman*. And I was on the phone with him as we tried to locate each other in the crowded terminal.

"Where are you?" he said.

"Right here."

Closer, closer. Our moment was near.

"I can't see you."

But I could see him. He stood about five feet away, so handsome, holding a single rose. Tears blinded me as the wheelchair rolled to within inches of him.

"I'm right here," I said.

He turned as I reached my arms up and around his neck and pulled him to me. Our first kiss was the sweetest and strongest I had ever tasted. We hugged; I didn't want to let go. After months of waiting we could finally inhale one another.

But one more moment was needed to consummate our relationship. We'd held off, deferred gratification, only singing it to each other on the phone with favorite songs, promising that the spoken word would be more meaningful when we could actually touch and look into each other's eyes.

"I love you, honey."

"I love you too."

Bonnie watched patiently, smiling, and then said, "Okay, you two. Let's grab our luggage."

JP drove us to the hotel in a rental car. My darling daughter was in the backseat and couldn't see me constantly touching my beau. The nearness of him was overpowering, and self-control had never been one of my stronger qualities.

All I could think about was the feel of his lips when we kissed and how I wanted more of that slow, sensual feeling. From the start he had been so wonderful and I knew we had a connection. Now, the crazy chemistry between us was undeniable.

By the time we got to the hotel it was late. Bonnie went to her own room, while JP and I walked to his. We had just enough time to shower before leaving for a dinner reservation that had been changed so many times during the day that we wouldn't be seated until 11 p.m.

To give me some privacy to freshen up and dress, JP went back to the lobby. When he returned he was wearing his sport coat and looked very dashing. I was in a black dress with gold shoulder straps.

"Wow, you're beautiful."

I blushed. I didn't think I was beautiful.

"But something is missing," he said. "Turn around and close your eyes."

My skin tingled to his touch. When he allowed me to open my eyes I discovered a gold and diamond double-heart necklace he had clasped around my neck. "Donna" was engraved on one heart,

"JP" was on the other.

I cried, of course. The scene was just like a jewelry commercial I'd seen on television and had deeply longed for--one of many fantasies that my online time with JP had inspired.

We kissed. It was a long, smoldering smooch that heated up the room. Our difference in height forced him to bend over and dominate me, and I clung to him so tightly I thought he might just push me down on the bed and take me. I was up for it. The heck with dinner. Room service would suit me just fine.

Fortunately, somehow we composed ourselves and found the restaurant where we enjoyed the most romantic dinner of my life. Candlelight, wine, and a very generous man whose eyes never strayed.

But now I faced a decision. Would I spend the night with JP in his room, or tip-toe into Bonnie's room?

We held hands as we left the restaurant, chatting. As the elevator climbed to our floor my heart fluttered. I wanted his lips on mine at least one more time before saying goodnight.

As we entered his room he tapped his iPhone and a loop of our favorite songs began their serenade.

"This magic moment" by the Drifters began to play.

Then we sat on the end of the bed and faced one another. I felt the urge to undress him, and hoped that he wanted to do the same with me.

Smiling, I inhaled deeply and put my hand on his.

"Well . . . now what?"

I knew the answer to my own question because we had rehearsed this moment in early August when we were still engrossed in our online chats.

With our lips very close we began to undress each other, kissing as we shed a skin. I unbuttoned his shirt, and he slipped the dress straps off my shoulders. Next I removed his belt and unzipped his pants so that he could stand and take them off.

John sensed that I was self-conscious about my body, so he

excused himself and went into the bathroom to brush his teeth as I stripped to my birthday suit and got under the bed covers.

In bed together, finally, we resumed the kiss we had started at the airport, and I rolled into his arms. My hands began exploring his body and he reciprocated, his touch so soft and gentle that we soon surrendered to a sensuous, unbridled love-making that continued until dawn.

Before we fell asleep, though, I was reminded of another online rehearsal, when all we could do was dream of actually feeling our bodies tucked together.

I fell asleep in his arms feeling completely safe and ... beautiful.

18

Donna/JP

We woke that first morning, curled together like newborns, as Debby Boone sang *You Light Up My Life*. My first impulse was to check my iPhone for a message from Donna, but as I wrapped her closer within my arms, I realized that was the last thing I needed to do.

She was right here.

It was real. We'd spent the night together making love, just like we'd imagined for the past couple of months. No longer did we wake up alone, but now we were two people folded into one.

My therapist had warned me I might not have a physical attraction; maybe there would be something about her that I wouldn't like. Managing my expectations, I suppose. But my attraction for Donna was strongly physical--which was a huge relief--and it was so much more. It was spiritual. Just like our finding each other online was an act of something bigger than us, so was my attraction to her. And she felt the same I was pretty sure.

I was prepared for what she looked like, we'd exchanged enough pictures. But I wasn't prepared for how good she'd make me feel. I wasn't prepared for the comfort and depth of love.

Especially when she started singing to me.

I thought I was dreaming: Debby Boone's beautiful voice, JP's arms around me, engulfing me in his warmth and scent, we'd spent the night making passionate love. It was too good to be true, and things that good never happen to me. But then I felt his lips on my neck. I interlaced my hands in his, and I knew it was real. I squirmed my hips closer to his.

The song finished and I heard my own voice singing. *You are my sunshine, my only sunshine.* It was the recording of me singing I'd sent John weeks ago. He must have added it to his playlist. I felt myself blushing. He'd actually kept it, and even added it to his iPhone.

As if reading my thoughts, he said, "I never had anybody sing to me before. Not my mother or my wife or kids, no one."

I squeezed his arms tighter around me and sang along. "You are my sunshine . . . " We giggled and he kissed my neck and ear and . . . we had to get up to meet the kids.

Damn.

We showered and dressed as the playlist gave us *Thousand Stars in the Sky* by Kathy Young, *Leaving on a Jet Plane, We Belong Together,* and others we both loved. It was the most perfect morning of my life.

We had to get downstairs to meet JP's son, Johnny, and his wife Bev. They'd flown in to meet everyone and it was all turning into a big do. All JP and I wanted to do was hang out in the bedroom and listen to music and make love. But Johnny and Bev being there gave Bonnie something to do, which gave JP and I more time together.

But before we went downstairs there was one more surprise and decision waiting for me.

"What are these?" I asked.

"Plane tickets."

JP smiled at my confusion and stroked my face.

"But I already have a ticket. Bonnie too."

"But those tickets will take you back both to Rochester, New York."

"Right. Where we live."

"But these tickets will take you to my home in Washington. Will you come with me, honey?"

The next four days we spent visiting the sites of Las Vegas, like the giant Welcome sign, where we took pictures of us. We saw *The Jersey Boys*, which was great because we both loved Frankie Valli and the music from that time. We played the slot machines and won a bit, lost a bit, and had romantic dinners too.

Most importantly, Donna and I got to know each other better, and we loved what we saw. We got closer, physically of course, but also just learning about each other and what we were like.

Our families gave us room to spend time together, except for one dinner where Bonnie showed up unexpectedly. She was having a good time getting to know Johnny and Bev and being some place other than Rochester, but she'd stopped by to say hi and see how we were. Eventually, Bonnie understood we wanted to be alone together and politely excused herself, chasing after other excitements. We were only too happy to forget the rest of the world, concentrate on each other, and let the romantic evening unfold.

That we could be so intimate so effortlessly made it feel as though we'd known each other for years. Donna told me she believed our cyber sex episodes online had prepared us for this.

That Friday, the second day we were there, JP took me to the drag races. When we were still texting online he'd told me all about his days competing in the Supergas class in the National Hot Rod Association (NHRA). While watching the races I imagined him winning the prestigious Division Championship in 2000. Back then he ranked third in the world. The world!

But I was realizing that he was the best at anything and everything he did, so the hot rod honors didn't surprise me. Standing beside him, absorbing his love of the cars and noise and speed, I felt so lucky to be part of his special world. It made me wish I'd been with him in those days too. But we were living other lives then. And while it felt as if we'd known each other forever, all I really cared about was the strong connection we had right then and there, at the races, in Vegas.

Although we spent a lot of time with our family, we had a lot of alone time together too. As much as we loved our kids, that was the best time. We hung out in our hotel room and listened to music or made love, or both. And when we slept we were always cuddled up together, like we couldn't get close enough. If one of us had to get up and go to the bathroom or get a drink of water, we'd return and kiss the other person on the neck, or back, or lips. We just couldn't get enough of each other. I still had to pinch myself sometimes to remind myself this wasn't a dream, it was real.

At Last. The song recorded by Etta James? That's how it felt, to me at least. At last I was with a man who adored me and willingly gave me his full attention and love.

Yet as our dream vacation was coming to a close, there was another important matter at hand.

When we woke up together after our first night in Las Vegas, JP had shown me the plane tickets to Washington state and asked, "Will you come with me, honey?"

I woke up the morning of November 2nd knowing I would go to Washington with JP rather than return home with Bonnie to Rochester. Maybe I'd known it all along, since that very first online text on July 28th. It seemed like a lifetime ago, and I guess it was, considering I was about to start a new life now.

But finally, after so many years of living a loveless life, I was with the man I loved and couldn't—-wouldn't--let him go. I didn't want to be without him ever again.

That morning Bonnie and I had stolen some time together after breakfast. So I put the big question to her.

"Are you sure it's okay with you if you go back home alone to Rochester? Without me?"

A little part of me wanted her to insist I come back home, that I couldn't just abandon her and chase off with this man. But instead, she did the right thing.

"Of course I want you to go with him, Mom," she said.

"But--"

"Mom, don't worry about me at all. You just go and be with this man that I know you love more than anyone in the world."

And so I did.

19

Donna/JP

By the time our flight from Las Vegas arrived at Tri-Cities Airport in Pasco, Washington it was dark, so Donna couldn't see much of the countryside. She would tell me later that she felt like she was in a daze. Or maybe this was a dream and she was hoping she would not wake up.

My son Steve and his wife Susie were there to greet us. I felt so proud and lucky that they were both very friendly and accepting of Donna; they each gave her a big hug.

Even with all the gentle fanfare, little did I know that while driving to the farm Donna wondered if she had done the right thing. Looking back, I thoroughly understand. I knew the surroundings; even in the dark I could imagine the landscape and my favorite spots. Even in the dark, I could find my way home.

Truth is, on the drive to a farm that was 40 minutes away from civilization, I too had concerns. Would Donna adjust? When living on Greenacres Road you couldn't just dash out the door on a moment's notice to pick up something at the grocery store. Unlike the city of Rochester, where virtually every retail need could be fulfilled within 5 minutes, the pace in my part of the world was slow, graceful. It took some planning.

On the other hand, I didn't live in Rochester. And while the online texts and the iPhone/FaceTime chats were exciting, they were always the next-best-thing to actually being there. So I had to hope that if she loved me, in time, maybe the familiarity of her former home would be replaced by her enjoyment of the abundant sprawl of the acreage and good people on my stretch of the road.

The greeting at the airport was warm, and that was reassuring, even if everyone in JP's family seemed about seven feet tall. I really had to stretch to return the hug.

But while in Las Vegas I had been challenged physically; I moved more in those four days than I had in recent decades. I was so tired that as we drove to the farm all I wanted to do was crawl into bed and hold my man. I loved being with him and touching him. He was the reason I'd taken so many leaps of faith in recent months.

Also, the long ride to the farm, in pitch dark, felt a bit bleak. All the more reason to want the comfort of his strong arms. Had I made the right decision?

When we walked into the farmhouse it was a bit like an old game show I recall watching years ago. The contestant is offered the choice of accepting whatever is behind curtain one, two, or three. That's when the big reveal occurred. The curtains would part and the contestant, in front of millions of people in the television audience, would either be thrilled or disappointed.

In this case, I was the only audience member and there was only one choice--my home. I believe I was more anxious than Donna.

We said our farewells to Steve and Susie, stepped onto the

porch and I unlocked the door. When we entered it was dark and Donna could see absolutely nothing. The moment of truth had arrived. I reached for the light switch and suddenly we were drenched in illumination.

Donna said, "Wow, this is awesome."

In one short sentence she had relieved the tension that was clutching my chest. This was a good beginning, I thought. She felt as though she had arrived in a place where she belonged and was welcome.

A bigger surprise awaited her when the sun came up the next morning. She looked out the window and saw the sprawl of 600 irrigated acres of farm fields that stretched as far as the eye could see. And, as the Broadway tune goes, "On a Clear Day" you could see Mt. Rainier, though it is about 150 miles in the distance.

Throughout the next days she started to rearrange a few things to her liking. It made me feel good that she was taking to her new surroundings, making her own nest.

From darkness comes light. Sounds Biblical. But so many miracles had already happened, I couldn't help but wonder, as JP unlocked the farmhouse door, if I dared ask for one more.

I held my breath. Then he flipped on the light. You already know what I said. But what did I see?

Shirley. JP's first wife was everywhere, in every stitch and measure. Her magic, her good taste, her way of making a good home.

I had to wonder if I was truly welcome here. It was a foolish question. Even Shirley, from the afterlife, seemed to embrace me. Remarkably, if I had decorated the home it would not have been much different. Shirley and I were on the same wavelength where style and comfort were concerned.

JP put his arms around me and said, "I hope you like it."

If Shirley had actually been in the room, I would have winked at her.

20

Donna

In the following days, I wandered through the rooms of the farmhouse, admiring every detail. Mostly it was the love inherent in every choice that was so moving. Certainly, any home will tell you something about the people who live there. This experience was different, more soulful. Shirley was still with us and despite an initial sense of welcome, I felt I should tread lightly even as I rearranged this and that.

Or maybe there was something more about my respect, and to a modest degree, my reticence about moving in too boldly.

On one occasion, I stopped in front of a mirror, surprised that another woman had arrived——me! LOL. As I looked me over, ever the prisoner of modesty, I had to ask, "Am I worthy of all this?"

I know, I know. There I go again, doubting myself and the miracle of chance that JP and I had experienced. In our first weeks of knowing one another I had balked at accepting simple gifts. Now, to be the lady of the house, so to speak, was such a blessing that I wanted to do right by it. I wanted to respect history, the history of the family that had thrived for decades in this wonderland, and then carefully, thoughtfully, make changes that sang to the arrival of new soulmates, Donna and JP.

The farmhouse at 2,500 square feet had plenty of space for the ghosts of the past and the new incarnation. The triple-wide mobile home structure boasted a beautiful kitchen, a den, living room, and dining room in an open-space layout. Although there were four bedrooms, we used two of them for His and Her offices.

All that walking I did in Las Vegas was good practice because JP enjoyed being outside and strolling through portions of the farm. They were eventful as I discovered all the things JP had talked about, such as the grass airstrip he maintained so that he could fly his single-engine Beech Bonanza to and from the farm.

As we explored the acreage we held hands and talked about my arrival in a place that had once been Shirley's domain.

JP's feelings of guilt would occasionally flare up, and it pained me to see him wrestling with his demons. It would take some time for all that to fade, even though my presence was exactly what he had wished for after meeting in Vegas.

My way of processing how fast we had fallen in love was to recall JP's online introduction.

> Lonely farmer: I recently lost my wife of 52 years and feel lost.
> I am 72 years old and just need someone to write to
> thanks for answering

Empathy and compassion were all I had to give him in the early days of our relationship. I knew in my heart that all I had wanted was to be helpful to a lonely person. If after supporting him through his grief we had parted ways, that would not have surprised me. So it goes. I was at peace with the way things happened.

One day while walking the farm, at every turn I could feel Shirley's presence and approval. It made me grin, which was not unusual for me at the time. After all, I was happy and in love. But JP saw my expression and asked, "What?"

We stopped and I looked up at this thoughtful, brainy, and at times, tortured man and said, "You know what, I like Shirley and I think she likes me too."

21

Donna/JP

"Fear of flying" was candy compared to what I felt. "Fear" for me meant sweaty palms, shaky vision, and a heart rate that was bound to put me in the hospital. As we walked along the grass runway toward his plane--his incredibly *small* plane--the ground actually tilted as I fought down my panic. JP grasped my hand.

"She's beautiful, isn't she?" he said, gazing lovingly at the overgrown tin can ahead.

"I . . . " Oh shit, now I couldn't speak! "I . . . I'm scared, honey." Whew, the words finally flew out.

He gripped my hand tighter. "I've been flying for [thirty] years, and I haven't died at it once."

Was that funny? I couldn't tell as I swiped the sweat rolling down my temple. I stumbled on a dirt clod.

"It's okay, Donna. It's a beautiful day with no wind. There won't be turbulence or any problems. We'll just do a little spin around the block."

Unable to laugh, I tried smiling but was pretty sure it looked instead like I'd just been bitten by something. I knew he had a pilot's license and was certified or whatever pilot's get. He'd been flying forever and was still excited about it as a little kid. Since our early days of getting to know each other online he'd talked about flying and driving his racecar. He loved them both, and who was I to get in the way of something he loved? But I hated flying on a good day, and now there was this miniature plane a few feet away, and I was supposed to climb in and take off? Yeah, right!

"I . . . I . . . " And there I was stuttering again. Maybe if I just clenched my fists and my jaw I could do this. I was stronger than this fear. But ooooooh noooooooo, it was so small!

I felt for Donna. I knew how afraid she was; her hand trembled in mine.

I also knew a lot of people feel that way when they get up in the air in a single-engine aircraft. The small fuselage is easily buffeted by the wind. That makes the experience feel precarious, though I remind passengers that it really is no different than riding in a boat through choppy waters and waves. The craft skims the top of the turbulence and adjusts to the environment. Also, if the weather isn't ideal, we don't take flight.

I love flying so much that I naturally wanted Donna to enjoy it too. We could go most anywhere in the region, if we wished. And the convenience could not be beat: the runway stretched along the side of the farmhouse. Since I knew all the driving we did to do simple chores was a big change for her, I played that angle.

"It's easy to take a little trip in the plane. We don't need to drive forty-minutes to the Tri-Cities Airport," I told her.

I'm a gambling man. I believed that if I could just get her up there once, I could show her how beautiful it was to be above everything, cruising along like a bird. I knew she'd love it. But first, I had to deal with that darn fear.

"You trust me, don't you?" I asked, trying the guilt angle first.

"Of course I do, sweetie," she said. "You know I trust you with everything, with my life. But that damn plane . . . I'm just afraid."

"You know that airplanes are safer than cars, right?" Maybe some statistics would work. "It's even safer than lightning. More people get struck by lightning than get killed in airplanes. Now when's the last time you got struck by lightning?"

I got a giggle. That was good. But her face was too red and her breathing fast.

"And you know I wouldn't let you down, right? I'd die myself before I ever hurt you."

She stopped and met my eyes. "I do, honey," she said. "I truly believe you and that's why I'm going to climb into that damn tin can and go flying with you. But it doesn't mean I have to enjoy it."

I gave her a kiss and then asked her to wait while I did my pre-flight inspection.

"I bet you'll end up loving it," I said as I began my routine. "Before long you'll be begging me to take you flying."

"Hah," she said. "And I'm the Pope. But I'm doing this for you, sweetie."

I walked the perimeter of the plane, inspecting the flaps and ailerons, and making sure nothing had damaged the antennas. I removed all the tie downs and rubbed my hand along the leading edge of the wing. I checked the fuel and oil quantities, and made sure the propeller didn't have any damage. It never did, but this was all part of a safety routine I'd had for decades, and it had kept me alive. I wasn't about to leave it out today of all days. When I was satisfied everything was as it should be, I helped Donna up a small ladder and onto the wing, where she waited while I entered the plane, and crawled across her seat to settled myself into the pilot's seat. Then I held my hand out and helped her into her own seat. Earlier, I'd bought a special cushion so that she could sit high enough to see out the window. Obviously, the plane wasn't constructed for people only five feet tall. It was only later that I learned that with all this maneuvering she had been terrified that she would fall off the aircraft and embarrass herself. But we took our time, and I talked her through it, until finally we were both seated inside and strapped in tight.

I gave her a grin and a kiss. "Today's a great day," I said, barely containing my excitement.

Here I was, all ready to go, and JP was taking forever with whatever he was doing. "Safety checks" he'd said. Well in the meantime I was dying with anxiety so how safe was that? But still he kept at it. Now that we were inside, he was going over every darn light and switch on the consol and moving the steering wheel back and forth as if he was figuring out how to use it. How was that supposed to help?

Finally, he placed some headphones on me and spoke through the mic. "How you doing, honey?" he asked.

"Dying," I said and shrugged. "Are we taking off today?"

He grinned then turned a knob, and a man speaking incomprehensible mumbo jumbo came over the headpiece.

"Weather's still great," said JP. He turned a switch and the engine growled and the propeller whipped its way around. As the engine noise grew, the entire plane lurched forward and back. I gripped the seat and squashed my eyes shut. "Ohhhhhhh, nooooooo," I squealed.

JP squeezed my hand then shifted his feet and we began to roll forward, bouncing on the soft grass.

"Hooooooooly shit!"

But he just grinned away, happy as a little boy, as he steered the plane down the runway past a pole with a limp windsock.

"It's a beautiful day to be flying," he said over the mic. "Not a thing to worry about, Donna. Just trust me, okay?"

I nodded rapidly and tried to unclench my teeth. The last thing I needed was to break a tooth out here.

We taxied to the end of the runway and JP nosed the airplane around so now the length of the runway stretched ahead. I swallowed my heart as he increased our speed. The plane bounced and roared and we headed for a collision with the tress at end of the runway, but still JP ploughed ahead. Faster and faster. I closed my eyes and my stomach dropped like I was in an elevator.

"Wheeeee!" he said. "We're up!"

I dared to open my eyes, and below me sped green Washington countryside. Higher and higher we flew until the ranches and farms were checkers criss-crossed with roads. He banked the plane and I screamed.

"Scared the hell out of me!" he said, still grinning like he'd won something.

"We'll tip over or crash or . . . something!"

"Nope." He patted my clenched hand. "We'll just loop the acreage and then head back in. It's just a little taste."

He carefully banked again until our nose was lined up with the length of the runway. This time I kept my eyes firmly shut until we were safely on the ground. But once we'd taxied to the hanger and he'd helped me down, I had to admit (to myself, not JP yet), that it was a thrill.

I couldn't help but wonder if Donna enjoyed the flight more than she let on. The mesmerizing birds-eye view of our home and surroundings gave me confidence. In time, I would encourage her to take in-flight pictures with her iPhone camera.

"Well, at least I got you smiling," I said as Donna stepped down from the plane.

"I'm drenched." She billowed her blouse in front.

"It'll dry, but you flew today. I'm so proud of you. Tomorrow, we'll try again. Maybe stay up a little bit longer."

"Tomorrow? What tomorrow? I'm not flying again tomorrow."

"Oh yes you are," I said and wrapped my arm around her. "One day you'll love this as much as I do. Just you wait and see."

And time it did take. Just like the phone, and just like getting

Donna to come meet me in Las Vegas, I knew she needed time. Time to get used to the flying and smaller plane, and time to build her trust in the flying.

But as stubborn as she was, so was I. So for the next few weeks I got her up in that plane as many times as I could. I even let her steer when we were flying straight and level. I figured if we extended each flight a bit it would seem normal to be so high. If she never truly adored the experience, that was OK. It was more an urge on my part to share the things that had fascinated me throughout my adult life.

Also, I teased her that if she would only fly with me there was one thing I would never ask her to do--ride in one of the high-speed cars I drove when I competed in the Supergas class of the National Hot Rod Association. There is no room for passengers in that type of rig.

I'm not sure she'll ever love the flying as much as I do, but she's more used to it now, and we can take trips to Sunriver whenever we want.

22

Donna/JP

Throughout our first weeks together, it wasn't just flying that we were adjusting too, but all kinds of quirks and nuances that you can only get to know when you're with someone in person, day-in, day-out. We had decades of life experience behind us and simply didn't have the same amount of hang-ups we used to. A gift from getting older is that so many things we used to worry about just didn't matter anymore.

Through our time together online and with the phone we already respected each other, and we were mature enough to lay anything we were upset about on the table and talk about it. I felt like I could talk to JP about anything, and it seems we did. Although I have to admit, he helped me sit down and discuss issues when I might have stuffed them down inside otherwise.

Like my Depends. I was so embarrassed about using them that I quickly shifted to Poise Pads.

"They're everywhere," said JP, searching through his sock drawer and pulling out another pad.

"I just need to make sure I have enough around, honey."

"But . . . everywhere? I found some in the closet the other day, and the bathrooms have them in every drawer."

The bathrooms was right. We had three of them. One for him. One for me. And one for us. I'd never had such luxury. But despite my pads hidden everywhere and my shame and shyness regarding my health issues that caused me to wear them, JP never once said an unkind word or did an unkind act. He was always generous and understanding, and I'm sure that's part of the reason that today I've lost over 200 pounds and don't have to wear the damn pads anymore.

I suppose when Donna moved in to live with me we went through what every new couple goes through as they get to know each other more intimately. Having been married to the same person for so long, I'd forgotten about those little things--like walking into the room naked. I simply couldn't do it at first. But Donna made me feel okay, just by saying the right things and being who she was.

"You're handsome and the man I love," she said.

"I'm old, and not half the man I was."

"I don't care. I think you're wonderful, all of you."

And I tried to do the same for her. If she undressed in front of me I always tried to make her feel beautiful and special. What I loved was watching her do her hair. I used to watch her get ready on Facetime, and now I could do it for real. She set up all her hair and perfume stuff in the room we made her office, and I'd go in there to be with her. No wonder she had a successful hair dressing business, she was amazing.

But I have to admit, not everything went as smoothly. For example, I guess I made a lot of decisions without checking in with Donna first. Like I might agree to go over to a friend's house for dinner without checking with her first. She wouldn't tell me why she was mad, so I encouraged her to discuss things with me. I just couldn't stand her holding things in and walking around being angry. Before, I had always been the one to make the decisions, but not with Donna. She wanted a say and rightly so. I liked the fact she wanted to help with making decisions.

And then there were her cold feet.

"They hurt they're so cold," I said once. "And rough too. Just put on some warm socks and sleep in those."

"Well, I have to put lotion on, so here, you can help." She handed me the bottle of lotion, and I rubbed her feet with them until they were warm and shiny. Then she slipped on the wooly socks and we cuddled all night long. Me on the right side, Donna on the left, of course. Some habits aren't made for breaking.

"Don't worry, sweetie," she said. "I'm used to sleeping on my recliner in the middle of the room, so either side works for me."

So in a way, we were making our own new habits. Designing our new life together. One that included a lot of talking and laughing and . . . Italian food. That I loved, but I could have done without all those vegetables!

"I'm not a rabbit," I said. "How do you expect me to eat all that green stuff?"

"Cheese," she said, and spooned some parmesan cheese on top. She was right too. Those rabbits don't know what they're missing.

The adjustments we both made were more about discovery than anything else. I learned that JP had a very focused one-track mind. Sometimes when he wasn't paying attention to me I would feel left out or ignored. Soon I realized that it was not indifference. The wheels of his very fine mind were turning. He needed that solitude to work through new plans or solve the riddles of life.

He too felt deserted when I'd close my office door and begin to write.

"What are you doing in there?" he asked, more than once.

He knew. I was recording as much as possible about our

relationship because I truly believed that the challenges we overcame might be helpful to others. The work was engrossing. I could lose myself in the memories and the expression of feelings that still amazed me--love, acceptance of a new way of life I never thought possible, a positive mind.

Despite all our shared interests--especially music but food, too, and frozen margaritas, old TV shows and movies-- learning to live together, day by day, also meant learning to live apart. Without fear that we would untether and wander in opposite directions never to be seen again.

Perhaps it was unrealistic to think we could always capture the magic we had experienced, the glee and utter devotion that comes with new love. If that was so, we also knew we didn't want to fall into old habits, such as notions of "wife" and "husband" and all that.

One thing I learned right off the bat was don't ever--ever!--sit next to JP when the Seattle Seahawks are playing. He got so excited he started punching and pushing me. Gently, of course, this was JP after all. But still. He got so worked up over their games!

In some ways he complicated my life more than ever before. He was generous with his money, but having a larger amount of money than I was used to was actually complicated. I was afraid to spend it.

"But I want you to treat yourself," he said. "Have some fun. You deserve it."

"But I love the dollar store," I said, which was true. "It's hard for me to just go out and spend money on myself."

But I also loved helping people financially, if I could. And that could get complicated too. Either way, JP was always so generous, which is part of why I loved him so much.

We connected at so many levels, and that's why we both assumed some higher power brought us together. But religion was another thing that brought up differences: JP was Mormon and I was Catholic. So we began going to both churches, JP's Mormon church one week, and my Catholic church the next week. Our religions entwined like voices, singers, it was another form of music that broadened our commitment to our improbable love affair.

As for marriage, that would eventually enter the dialogue. Was it a step we wanted to take? Was it even necessary in this oh so modern world?

No need to rush. One step at a time. We were already blessed.

We soon became two peas in a pod. We developed a new life together, one that was uniquely our own. He was hard of hearing, so I was his ears. And I had trouble focusing, so he kept me on track. If something upset either one of us, we talked about it. So despite some bumps and hiccups over those first few weeks, we just continued to get closer and closer.

23

Donna/JP

That first November, Donna and I drove to my condo in Sunriver, Oregon. I was excited to show her the magnificent beauty of the place and that for the rest of our lives we would have it to enjoy. Shirley and I had bought the place just a short time before she died, so I'd never used it much. Still, signs of her were everywhere: her bike and helmet and clothes and even food in the refrigerator. I have to admit, that first visit was awkward in that way.

Donna sensed Shirley's presence too, and in the most respectful way she began to change things around. Just enough so that over time it became our place, Donna's and mine. Shirley's presence remained, but in an approving way. It was as if she was saying, "Donna is a wonderful woman who's making you very happy and you have my blessing."

The first time Donna rode Shirley's bike I got a bit sad. But at the same time, it was the moment when I realized my old life was over. This was my life now, with Donna by my side, and I truly believed Shirley was okay with it.

It got so that it seemed like Shirley was speaking to me through Donna. I don't know how that all works, but sometimes Donna would say or do exactly what Shirley would have said or done. It felt like it was how Shirley communicated to me that she was happy for me. Which is all part of our spiritual connection and continued to fuel our belief that a higher power was at work.

The first time JP told me about Sunriver I didn't understand what he was talking about. A river? In the sun? And to make it more confusing, every time he mentioned it he talked about a king size bed. So when we went to visit that first time, I was curious and maybe just a little apprehensive too.

I quickly learned that talking about Sunriver and experiencing it were two completely different things. Keep in mind that I'm not a very athletic person. Exercise for me might have been a nice walk or maybe a class in the gym, years ago. Sunriver, on the other hand, was an all inclusive resort complex with about thirty miles of biking and walking paths. They had bocce ball courts, horseback riding, canoeing, kayaking, dancing, three pools, and even a golf course. They had morning and evening restaurants, a night club, and an amphitheatre where they booked stars like the Temptations. It was magnificent.

I couldn't believe I had a wonderful new first home in Washington, and now I had a second home too. How could I justify all of it? How could I deserve all this? So that first visit I was uncomfortable. And then there was Shirley's presence everywhere. I admit it wasn't a bad feeling, more like a loving, comforting one. But still I wondered how I would fit in. That first time I wondered if it was me or Shirley there. But the strangest thing was, it was like Shirley was somewhere inside of me. JP noticed it too. I'd say something and he'd say, "That's exactly what Shirley would have said!"

How could that be? Thank God she was a wonderful loving woman. Imagine if she'd been a terrible witch? But then JP wouldn't have been with her for his entire life. It all works that way, and I had nothing to worry about.

We drove to Sunriver in JP's Corvette and brought back his

Chevy Traverse, a big SUV type car. JP let me drive the Corvette part of the way there and it was fantastic. Holy cow I was driving a Corvette! Every time I had a new accomplishment like this I would cry. JP would feel bad but I just explained I was so happy. It was all so unbelievable.

For our next visits sometimes we drove and sometimes we flew his little plane, which I was getting more used to by now. We'd take off from our own airstrip on Greenacres Farm and then land on Sunriver's strip. Half the time I figured I must be dreaming. It was all so good. How had this all happened to me after all those years of misery?

The time at Sunriver also allowed us to trade wide open spaces for a tighter community life. I could introduce Donna to the friends I had there. Those meet and greets went well, further deepening my belief that I had been wise to court Donna as I had. We were such great companions, and everyone loved her personality and enthusiasm.

Another issue on my mind was Donna's driving ability. Due to health and immobility issues, Donna had not driven for several years. I believed the Chevrolet Traverse at the condo would be a better vehicle for her to tune up her driving skills. We went out for little trips in the area and she did very well. And on the drive back to the farm, she willingly took the wheel for a portion of the journey.

24

Donna/JP

The welcoming parties, family dinners and breakfasts at the farmhouse, continued throughout the month. It gave us all time to get acquainted and develop some comfort with everyone in my circle. Thanksgiving at the home of one of my granddaughters was a highlight. Our first major holiday together.

The next challenge was preparing for a Christmas trip to Rochester. Now it was my turn to be introduced. I'd met some important people in Donna's life during our FaceTime conversations. Now we would be face to face, and I was thoroughly excited when we arrived——and very surprised.

I had no idea how vast Donna's family tree was. She had cousins everywhere. And brothers, daughters and their partners, a circle of dear friends and, of course, her mother. They all welcomed me with open arms, and as it turned out, we all got along so well.

Our stay lasted ten days. We experienced some balmy weather——65 degrees in December——and so took a day-trip to Niagara Falls, a 50-mile drive. It felt like a honeymoon. And the falls were a truly amazing sight to behold.

But the big moment was Christmas Eve. Santa Claus (Donna's brother) arrived early and handed out gifts to all the children. It touched me to see the little faces glowing, so thrilled and grateful for their simple gifts. It made me reflect on the many Christmases I'd spent with my family.

Shirley and I had had enough financial security to be generous with our children, but there were times when I believed it was out of balance: Too commercial; too much about material wealth and expensive, beautifully wrapped presents under the tree.

I was humbled to see Donna's family revel in the joy of being together and sharing what they could. The paradox was vivid to me: Just because I had more money than Donna did not mean I was providing anything more valuable than what she was giving to me.

It was Christmas Time when I finally realized God's love for me. My whirlwind trip to Las Vegas and then Washington State was the first time in my life that I had ever been away from home, so returning for the holidays was a new experience.

My family welcomed JP and I at the airport. They threw their arms around me, which was no surprise. But their hugs and kisses were also generously shared with JP. They all wanted a piece of him, a moment, a word. But I wouldn't let go of my knight. I was just so proud and humbled and happy. We stood there crying. Joyous. Celebratory. Close as close can be.

The next day, after a good night's sleep, we visited my mom. I was sixty-eight years old and yet it was comforting to know that my childhood home still existed, even my bedroom. Through the years, the house had provided a sense of security for me, knowing that if I failed at life I would always have a place to go.

The homecoming made me realize what was missing in Washington at JP's farm. Surely, I was comfortable there and loved. But I no longer had the whole family protection plan working for me. That was why I was sometimes blue wandering through the farm house. How could I have left my family, my foundation? And had my absence caused my mom and siblings to suffer that same gnawing, empty feeling?

Yet a moment later, surrounded by my family and the love

of my life, and everything seemed okay, like I was exactly where I was meant to be. The puzzle was now complete. That's what I meant by saying God's love was suddenly so apparent. He gave me this. He was telling me, I believe, this is where you belong. This state of grace.

So, when it was time to head back west, we waved goodbye and boarded our plane. We were both glad to get back to the farm house in Washington.

As we turned off Greenacres Road into our driveway, I turned to JP.

"There's no place like home, eh?"

His face warmed to a big, loving smile. It was obvious how much those words meant to him. He had done everything in his power to make me comfortable in the house he had shared for so many years with Shirley. He had succeeded, and I wanted him to know that.

"You didn't want to stay in Rochester? Just a little longer?" he asked.

"At first I had a pang. Seeing everybody, Christmas and all that. They're my family. But then I realized, that was the old me. The new me lives with a stud muffin on a big farm in the Evergreen State. In the middle of nowhere."

"In the middle of somewhere."

"Forever where."

He laughed. We kissed.

The trip back to Rochester had been a lot of fun. But the best part was knowing that the reason our journey turned out so well was because I *didn't* want to stay. It was a much-needed visit. A blessing. Now it was time to unpack another gift——more time with my man.

When JP unlocked the front door of the farm house I walked across the threshold and felt as if I'd just been lead to an expanse of sweeping hills and blue skies. Birds sang and the sun warmed us. I belonged here. *We* belonged here.

25

Donna/JP

When Donna and I first started texting she told me that she used to be a ballroom dance instructor. I always had a desire to learn how to dance but never did anything about it. Jokingly, she said she would teach me. But the 2,500 hundred miles between us made that impossible.

That changed after Las Vegas. We began the lessons, even though I didn't know if I could learn because I'd always thought that I had two left feet.

Thankfully, I had a good teacher. Little by little, I made progress. We practiced every chance we had. It seemed the perfect metaphor for us. Somehow, we had swept through many obstacles, doubts and grief with the grace of Fred Astaire and Ginger Rogers.

Then we learned that there would be a Valentine's Day dance at Sunriver with a 20-piece band. We had to go. God, what fun. We danced all night. Despite being worried that I would look like a fool, I believe I did just fine.

I began giving him dance lessons at the farm, just as I had promised. He did quite well, right off the bat, and he was eager to continue with more lessons every day for at least thirty minutes.

Sunriver was a blast, but we had an even bigger challenge when we returned to Las Vegas. Freemont Street is where all the action is. People dance in the street to a variety of bands and music. We were surrounded by adults of all ages, each couple energized by the pulse of performers.

It was easy for me to say that I hadn't danced like that in twenty years. Of course not; I'd suffered too many physical problems and indignities. Yet JP's love had helped me adjust my diet and lose weight. (And I did tell him early on in our relationship that I wanted to be "naughty.") Now we were dancing like a couple of sixteen-year-olds, and that too was healthy and invigorating. Swing music, 1950s hits, Broadway tunes and jazz.

Sweating but giddy, I said, "I haven't danced like that in ..." I couldn't finish my sentence, so JP did.

"In twenty years?" Then he quipped, "Heck, I haven't danced like that——ever!"

He had a real knack for it. He was so good with the steps that he took over and began to lead me, as though he was the teacher. That's how great he is at everything he does. Nothing is too big to conquer.

That's probably why we were totally unprepared for the emergency we experienced months later. We'd been living as close to a fairy tale as anyone could. Yet everything casts a shadow. Even happiness.

26

Donna/JP

The bleeding began at night after I'd woken up with a full bladder, relieved myself in the bathroom, and then returned to bed. The first sensation was a wet face. I couldn't understand it, so I turned on the beside lamp, brought my fingers to my nose and mouth and discovered blood. Everywhere. Lots of blood. On my body, the bed clothes, the floor.

I used to constantly think about illness and death. After all, I'd had two bouts with cancer, and various other chronic health problems. Any and every ache, pain or unexpected physical discomfort frightened me.

"JP, I'm dying. Wake up. Please. I'm dying. Call an ambulance!"

He jolted upright as the blood continued to gush and then run down my throat. When he put his hands on me he could feel my body shaking. It was terror: I knew I would be dead before the emergency medical people arrived. The distance was too great. It took forty minutes to get anywhere in the vast farmlands of Washington State.

JP grabbed his phone and dialed 9-1-1. His voice was calm but urgent.

During our Christmas vacation in Rochester, we'd cuddle in the bed of our hotel room and talk about our "perfect love." We'd recount how we had found each other, each brave step that had brought us closer——2,500 miles closer——so that we could touch each other and kiss.

We also marveled at how well we both fit into our new extended family. Bliss. We could spend the rest of our lives together.

"I don't want to die now! I don't want to die!"

"You're going to be okay. Just——"

"I need to be in a safe place! I don't want to——"

JP ran to the bathroom for a towel, then softly pushed it against my nostrils as he tried to wipe away the deluge with the long corners of the terrycloth.

"It'll stop, it'll stop," he soothed.

But it didn't. The red flood just kept coming.

JP did a good job of keeping me talking, trying to refocus my thoughts. But all I could think was, I'm cursed. I'll never escape it. All my negativity is coming back to get me. I'm going to bleed to death in a remote, rural grave.

The first faint sound of a siren shut me up. The vehicle would arrive much sooner than I'd expected. Was the tide turning?

JP left me to open the front door, and in came the paramedics with their equipment and stretcher to cart me away. I was surrounded by capable people, who understood that time was crucial. They asked questions, tapped my veins and medicated me. One face was familiar, and that was comforting. She was a neighbor, a new friend.

But the others were all strangers. In an instant, my gut cramped with a terrible, grief-stricken yearning for my family. Only they could understand what I was about to lose. Only they could appreciate that I'd finally found the love of my life after hiding from romance and affection for years, inside my dark cloud of self-pity and doubt.

"Call them, JP."

"Who?"

"Mom. My brothers. I want to talk to——"

"Let's go!"

The EMTs lifted me onto the gurney and began to roll me out to the ambulance. The emergency lights sprayed the out-buildings and shot through the midnight dark, licking the fallow fields and silhouette of Mt. Rainier——the wonders of nature I might never see again.

From then on, all I remember is speed, my body strapped to the gurney, looking out the rear window of the emergency vehicle. I saw headlights. Two intense yellow eyes staring at me the whole time it took to get to the hospital.

I couldn't bear another loss. More grief would surely kill me. Thinking of my own needs, though, would not help Donna.

As the ambulance pulled out of our driveway and sped down Greenacres Road, I sprinted for my Silverado pickup truck.

Quick starts were my specialty, I reminded myself. There was a time when speed and the lust for achievement earned me a Division Championship in the Supergas class in the National Hot Rod Association. I knew how to get my rig in gear and on the path to glory——fast.

The red tail lights of the emergency vehicle grew closer as I overcame the distance between us. I wanted to all but kiss the bumper of that van so that my headlights would beam through the rear window. Donna needed to know that she was not going to leave me behind. No, ma'am. Not so fast, honey. I'm right behind you.

As I charged into the hospital I shook my head clear and, internally, barked an order: don't let her see your fear.

In the ER Donna wanted her family by her side. She missed them so much, and that made me hurt, in a way, to know that I was no replacement for them. She was like a little girl, away from home for the first——and maybe dying. I couldn't blame her for feeling the way she did. I did everything in my power to comfort her, but it wasn't enough.

Doctors and nurses packed Donna's nose with absorbent materials and did some tests.

Donna kept insisting, "But I've never had a bloody nose in my life."

That fact didn't matter. This was no normal bloody nose. It took hours to stop the bleeding.

Slowly, the sense of crisis waned and our spirits cautiously lifted. Donna and I began to breathe easy, inhaling the fragrance of tomorrow and the next day . . . and the next.

The doctors would release Donna from the hospital that night with instructions to keep her nostrils stuffed for three days.

The diagnosis? The climate Donna now lived in was extremely dry compared to Rochester. The episode was startling to me for so many reasons. Most of all, I promised myself never to forget what my love had left behind to be by my side.

27

Leap Year

In the months that followed, as JP and I continued to become accustomed to each other, and most importantly, as we were constantly reminded of how much we loved each other, we would hint at getting married. No one made any grand statements, but I might tease him about being a good husband, and he might counter with, "Well, when we get married, you'll see who's boss." All in jest, all in fun. But with an undercurrent of truthfulness and longing.

It turned out it was leap year, and one day I remembered that that's the year that girls can ask boys to dances, dates, and . . . the wedding chapel. So I made a joke to JP and actually asked him to marry me. We both laughed and carried on as if nothing important had happened. Which it hadn't. Not yet, anyway.

Then near the end of February, it might even have been the 28th, I was in my new office in my new home with JP when he came to see me. He approached my desk, all business-like, swung my chair around, dropped onto one knee, and said. "Donna, will you marry me?"

The first thing I did was burst into tears. Then between the blubbers and sniffles I told him, "Yes, of course I will, honey."

"Then I'd better get on the phone and ask your mother for permission."

I giggled at this, but he picked up the phone and dialed my mother. "Mom," he said. "I love your daughter more than anything in the world, and I'd like to ask you for her hand in marriage."

I could hear everything, and at this point she paused as if to think about it. I swear, JP's face turned purple. But then she laughed and told him of course he could. Like any great mom, she was just happy that I was happy, and she knew how happy JP made me.

From that point on we began planning our wedding. We wanted it to be a big party and invite both our families and friends. Somehow we landed on April 8th, 2017 as the day, and we'd have the wedding in New York.

Or at least that's what we thought

Long before I asked Donna to marry me, I knew I wanted to spend the rest of my life together. And I guess it really didn't take us long to get around to it, considering we'd only lived together for a few months when I finally asked her. But in our own way, we took our time getting there. First through playing and joking, which had become our style, and then through making the decision and getting on with it.

The last bit, however, wasn't turning out to be as easy as we thought. We wanted to have a big wedding; to let the entire world know about our love for each other and join the celebration. But because our families were on opposite ends of the country, one side would have to do most of the traveling. I figured my family would love to have the opportunity to go to New York, but it quickly became apparent it wouldn't be as easy as we'd hoped. Everybody had jobs, and families, and traveling wasn't cheap. Donna and I both began to feel uneasy about the plan. We weren't going to not get married, we were rock solid on that, but we needed an easier way for everyone to take part.

One day a few months after I proposed, my granddaughter invited Donna and I to their wedding. Only this was no ordinary wedding--they were eloping. Up in Coeur d'Alene, Idaho a place called the Hitching Post conducted weddings with no fuss or frills.

The idea of eloping plucked a heartstring and sent me smiling. "JP," I said. "We're going up that way to buy a car anyway. Why don't we skip all this fuss and just elope too? We could do it on July 28th, the very same day we met online, and one year later. We can have a party in New York on April 8th, and that'll make it easier for everybody."

"But don't you want a wedding?" he asked. "I mean, a real one? I want to do that for you."

I placed my hands on his cheeks and kissed him. "This would make me happiest of all, honey," I said. "I'd love to get married just the two of us. On our own. It will be so romantic, and we can have a big 'ol party afterwards."

He realized how much I wanted to get married this way, and all he wanted was for me to be happy, so that's what we decided to do. We both knew we were in this relationship for the long haul, and we spent lots of time talking and dreaming, but at our age time is of the essence. Our love wasn't about careers or castles, but rather it was a model to those around us demonstrating a marriage that shone the light and love we share. It all became so perfect that JP and I figured it was a sign from above when his granddaughter told him where they were getting married.

And funny enough, another sign from above arrived soon thereafter, in the form of the bishop from JP's Mormon church knocking at our door. We were happy to see him, but a bit confused too, because I guess he didn't stop by often.

"I don't actually know why either," he'd said. "I was driving by and just felt a calling to turn up your road and come visit."

We chatted for awhile, and then I remembered that my mother had reminded me that very morning to get my engagement ring from JP blessed.

"Well, why you're here," I said, "and even though I'm Catholic, would you mind blessing my engagement ring?"

Of course, he didn't mind a bit. And even though the bishop did not pronounce us man and wife, it felt like a union had officially been recognized. Two loving people had merged in still yet another way.

On the drive up to the Hitching Post, Donna and I talked about how we didn't know how many days we had in front of us. But what we did know for sure, and had known for a long time now, was that we wanted to spend whatever time we had left together. With so fewer days ahead than behind, why not get married? Why not live our lives to the fullest while we still could? We wanted to be together traditionally and spiritually too, and that meant tying the knot--even if that meant eloping on the way to buy a new car.

We pulled up quietly in the parking lot of the Hitching Post. I helped Donna out of the car, and we held hands as we walked up to the door.

The Hitching Post is located in the idyllic town of Coeur d'Alene, Idaho. It sits nestled between rolling hills and just down the road from the world renowned Lake Coeur d'Alene. We entered and walked between rows of seats right up to the altar, where Reverend Lynn was waiting for us. We'd already got our marriage licenses across the street at the County Clerk's Office, and all we had left to do was say our vows in front of this soft-spoken, gentle woman.

The ceremony was quaint and personal, and of course I cried through the whole thing. This had all happened so fast that my rings were still being sized. So we used my great-grandmother's ring instead. It had been handed down for generations and now it was my turn.

Any concerns weren't about what we were doing, but about what others would think of it. Until I turned to JP and said, "Who gives a damn."

We laughed, said our vows amidst the flowers and peacefulness, and were married

Afterword

OMG! You Met on the Internet?
https://www.facebook.com/LoveWillFindYou2

Did you find love in an unexpected way or place?
Did love find you when you least expected it?
Please join our Facebook community
and share your story.
The love you need is out there.
Believe!

Acknowledgements

We'll always remember the support and encouragement we received from our extended families and friends. Our unexpected journey was sudden, full of wonder and, at times, tinged with doubt. They helped us understand that when love happens—go with it.

This memoir would not have been possible without the guidance and storytelling skills of two talented writers and publishing consultants. Heartfelt thanks to Karen Lacey and Douglas Glenn Clark.

http://theuncommonoctopus.com/
http://www.exclusiveghost.com/

www.ingramcontent.com/pod-product-compliance
Lightning Source LLC
Chambersburg PA
CBHW061432040426
42450CB00007B/1022